Native Advertising

Native Advertising

The essential guide

Dale Lovell

KoganPage

First published in Great Britain and the United States in 2017 by Kogan Page Limited

2nd Floor, 45 Gee Street	c/o Martin P Hill Consulting	4737/23 Ansari Road
London	122 W 27th Street	Daryaganj
EC1V 3RS	New York, NY 10001	New Delhi 110002
United Kingdom	USA	India

© Dale Lovell 2017

ISBN   978 0 7494 8116 2
E-ISBN   978 0 7494 8117 9

British Library Cataloguing-in-Publication Data

A CIP record for this book is available from the British Library.

Typeset by Integra Software Services, Pondicherry
Print production managed by Jellyfish
Printed and bound in Great Britain by CPI Group (UK) Ltd, Croydon CR0 4YY

CONTENTS

PART FIVE The future of native advertising 199

For Chloe and Eleri

ABOUT THE AUTHOR

Dale Lovell is the UK Managing Director and Chief Digital Officer at ADYOULIKE, a worldwide leader in native advertising technology. Based in London, he works with leading brands and their agencies running native advertising campaigns with some of the world's largest media publications.

Dale has worked in journalism, digital publishing, content strategy and creative content marketing for over 16 years. Prior to ADYOULIKE, Dale was co-founder of Content Amp, a content marketing distribution service. A regular blogger, columnist and speaker on native advertising, Dale also sits on the Internet Advertising Bureau (IAB) UK's Content and Native Advertising Council. In 2015 he was listed as a BIMA Hot 100.

ACKNOWLEDGEMENTS

They say it takes a village to raise a child. The same is true for any book on marketing today. The pace of change that technology is bringing to the way business is done means that there are no longer any experts. I'm not one, certainly. Even on a topic such as native advertising in which I've invested a large amount of my time – and have been a part of from the very beginning – it's difficult to claim expertise. Knowledge, yes. But an expert? Change is so rapid that you are likely to be left red-faced and wrong-footed relatively quickly if you espouse your expertise for too long in this game.

I prefer to describe myself as an interested party. I'm inquisitive, for sure.

So when it came to writing a book about native advertising my inquisitiveness naturally led me to quiz my friends, colleagues and contacts working in the space for their take on this thing we call native advertising.

Without contributions this book would never have taken shape. So I'm thankful for all of you who I have nagged and harassed into making a contribution. The views of those working in publishing, advertising, ad tech and policy, from around the world, have helped make this book a far richer experience for readers than I could have hoped to achieve alone. I'd like to thank, in no particular order, the below for their personal contributions:

Augustin Croll, Jesper Laursen, Michael Villaseñor, Jamie Toward, Justin Choi, Hannah Meium, Daniel Emery, Clare O'Brien, Piers North, Melissa Wusaty, Kolja Kleist, Damian Ryan and Claire Austin.

Special mention must go to Michael Villaseñor, *New York Times*, who went above and beyond the call of duty in securing an interesting case study. So too to Clare O'Brien for listening to my original book idea, offering some insightful direction, as well as a great written contribution on measurement. Melissa Wusaty also deserves extra thanks for an invaluable in-depth contribution on the role of content and the changing role of content marketing.

A big, big thank you to Damian Ryan, not only for his contribution to this book, but more importantly in helping me get the book off the ground in the first place. For the glowing introduction to Kogan Page, eternal thanks. Thanks to the team at Kogan Page who helped on the book too – Jenny Volich and Charlotte Owen, in particular. Your support was much needed in guiding this book to completion.

On a wider note I'd like to thank all of my advertising and publishing contacts that contributed with recommendations for topics, case studies, interview leads and research material – without this assistance this book would be far less insightful. Thanks to Ben Atkinson and Sandro Del Grosso at ESI Media for the case study contributions, too.

I'd also like to thank everyone at ADYOULIKE – in the UK, France and the US. For our investors, staff, customers and publisher partners: this book is as much your story as my own. In particular, I'd like to thank ADYOULIKE co-founders Julien Verdier and Yohan Elmaalem, my business partners, friends and colleagues with a united goal to grow native advertising worldwide and make our shared business a global success.

Obviously, special mention must be given to my long-standing business partner, Francis Turner. I would not be writing this book without him. As I set out in the introductory chapter, it was Francis who introduced me to native advertising in the first place. Since then we've embarked on an incredible journey together into the heart of native advertising. Remarkably, we are still friends, too! In most of the personal stories I share in this book, Francis was there too (sometimes cringing at my actions!). Francis's understanding of how native advertising fits into the wider digital ad market is second to none. I can think of no one whose opinion I'd prefer to have on these topics. Francis and I share a lot of the same opinions on native advertising, though these words (and the royalties – nice try Francis) are my own.

I'd like to thank my parents, for their continued support, and for instilling in me the appetite for hard work that I needed in order to complete this book while also managing a busy business. To all my friends and family who have offered me encouragement and support over the years, many thanks.

My wife, Chloe, deserves special credit. Chloe has not only had to shoulder all of the child care duties while her husband was off writing 'his book' at weekends and evenings, but she was also roped in as a sub-editor and proofreader as submission deadline day drew near. Her assistance has been much needed and appreciated. But Chloe has also had to contend with the distracted, private insecurities and yo-yo-ing mood of a first-time book writer in the process. Without her support and reassurance, I might not have made it to deadline day. Thank you.

Lastly, a thank you to the coffee shops of Windsor, where I live, who played host to this strange, hulking, bearded man, who sat in the corner furiously tapping away at his laptop for hours on end, nursing endless cups of coffee, for many a weekend and evening. For the free Wi-Fi and laptop charge, I'm thankful.

PART ONE
What is native advertising?

What is native advertising?   01

A definition

Native advertising is a form of paid media where the advertisement is relevant to the consumer experience, integrated into the surrounding content and is not disruptive.

Native advertisements look and feel like the content that surrounds them. They are described as native because the advertising looks and behaves just like the editorial content around it. The ads sit within the editorial feed sections of websites and the ad works in the same way as existing editorial; for example, you normally will have to click on the content in order to interact with it.

Introduction 02

My story

It was early in 2012. My business partner, Francis Turner, and I were sat in our office in Windsor, just outside London, where we ran our content and distribution start-up, Content Amp. We had launched in 2010 and it was completely self-funded by the two of us. We had nine or ten employees at the time – all recent graduates – huddled into a small office space that was probably only really suitable for half that number. It was very much a start-up's start-up.

Our business focused on creating content on behalf of brands and helping them distribute and share it to relevant blogs and publications. It was a business that was part content marketing, part blogger outreach, part influencer marketing and part search engine optimization. We were profitable and growing. But we also recognized the limitations of content creation – it was difficult to scale, particularly with no investment or funding behind us. We loved the content marketing space and were passionate about the market, but we were looking for something to set us apart, to help us grow.

Then we discovered native advertising. Or rather Francis did. It was Francis who regularly kept his eye on emerging US advertising trends, not me. He shared some online marketing articles with me from the US that were littered with a new phrase: native advertising. We ran through the articles together. Both of us had over 10 years' digital marketing experience – Francis in ad sales, ad tech and ad networks, myself in digital content, publishing and digital marketing. We read more and more, researched and discussed.

We both instinctively understood the mechanics of this native advertising world: we could see how the advertising was created, why it had developed and how it fitted in with the wider content marketing trend in digital that we were a part of. Crucially with our backgrounds in ad tech, content and publishing, we could see the fit for our business – and the huge opportunity, too.

We were excited. It seemed the perfect fit to our partnership – content with advertising; creativity with network-level scale. The more we researched, the more we liked. We realized quickly that despite being one of the most digitally savvy and advanced advertising markets on the planet, no one was talking about native advertising in the UK. No one was making a move in the space. After a few short months of investigating, we decided to pivot our business towards native advertising. So began my adventure.

Things moved quickly from there. We needed technology to develop the native proposition in the UK. We had our single developer in the business look into it in more detail. We went out looking for venture capital – meeting scores of would-be investors along the way. Everyone we met liked the proposition, but we got the feeling most of them were a little apprehensive about such a new market.

But one of the venture capitalists we met with, Philippe Herbert from Banexi Ventures (now Kreaxi) in Paris, happened to be the initial investor in ADYOULIKE, a Paris-based native technology platform that was really championing the native advertising space in France. They were on our radar.

We agreed to meet. In co-founders Julien and Yohan we immediately had a rapport. We saw in them some like-minded entrepreneurs that spoke exactly the same language as we did on native advertising. They, like us, recognized the amazing market opportunity. After a few more months of getting to know each other, our businesses, and some negotiations, of course, Content Amp became ADYOULIKE. That was in March 2014.

In the process we created the UK's first – and Europe's leading – in-feed native advertising technology company. Since then we have helped grow the European market for native advertising to become close to a $10 billion-a-year industry. With offices in Paris, London and New York, our business – from humble beginnings as plucky start-ups in France and the UK – now operates in a burgeoning global market at the cutting edge of marketing, advertising and technology.

But the really exciting part is that the native advertising market is still only in its infancy. Native advertising impacts all of our lives: anyone with a smartphone almost certainly interacts with native advertising on a daily basis. The native advertising market is estimated to be worth $59 billion by 2018 and $85.5 billion by 2020. It is the medium all advertisers will need to adopt – and understand – over the coming years for success.

Native advertising: digital's indigenous ad format

I believe that 'native advertising' – although the term comes from the advertisement matching the look and feel of the editorial surrounding it, in that it is native to the publication it sits on – is actually better used as a term to describe the advertising format that is indigenous – native – to online. Native advertising is digital's ad format. I am convinced of that.

Think about it. Banner ads were essentially adopted by early websites to replicate the standard ad blocks seen in newspapers. A banner says, 'This is where the ads can sit – in these standard block units.' Video ads, even still today, are quite often repurposed TV ads. All are formats that came before the advent of the internet.

Native advertising is different. Like the digital medium itself, native ads take elements from other media, but utilize them correctly for the digital world. Native advertising in my opinion is the first 'native' advertising format of the digital world. We are barely 20 years into mass internet usage, and far, far less for mobile browsing; in my mind, native advertising is the format all future digital advertising will take. This book will show you why and how.

The journey of digital advertising

Native advertising is in part a consequence of and reaction to some major digital consumer trends – mobile, social media, video, content, ad blocking, the decline in print, and many smaller and subtler changes. Within this book I will look to touch upon them all – and more. We'll get into the nitty-gritty heart of what you need to know about running a native advertising campaign yourself. But we'll also look at issues such as fake news, ad fraud and the wider digital media economy – issues that are not specific to native advertising, but areas that you need to know if you are trying to understand the spirit of native advertising.

It's only when you look at the journey that digital has taken over the last 20 years that it all suddenly clicks into place. So when it came to writing a book about native advertising, I quickly realized that in order to tell the story of native advertising properly – and if I was to succeed with the aim of fully explaining why it's important, and why its success as a medium is inevitable – I would need, in part, to tell the story of digital as a whole, too.

For some people native advertising is the solution that digital publishing has been waiting for – the format that will transform the fortunes of struggling digital publishing business models and usher in a new golden age in publishing. For others it's a symbol of the death of publishing as we know it, the death of editorial independence and the last-ditch – 'dead cat bounce' – effort of an industry that has been searching for a business model for 20 years or more, and failing.

Evolution not revolution

But native advertising is fundamentally not a revolution in advertising – despite what many vested interests may try and tell you. It's an evolution. It is a medium born out of major changes in consumer habits online. It's the evolution of advertising formats for a mobile-first world. It's the evolution of advertising content for a world that is continuously engaging with the feed, where interruption is only OK if you do it in an entertaining or informative way. It's the evolution of publishing and platform revenue models for publishers that can no longer afford to rely on dwindling returns from print. It's the evolution of the newsroom and editorial jobs. It's a technology that can actually help against ad blocking and help distribute the countless pieces of content brands that publishers are creating on a daily basis. I feel privileged and excited to be a part of these changes.

I work in native advertising. I've researched it, written about it and practised it. I've also tried looking at it from afar, putting it in perspective in terms of what has come before it and what the future holds – all of which we will cover in this book.

In this book I aim to outline exactly what native advertising is, diving deep into the various categories of native and how these can work for your organization. I'll also offer up first-hand advice from my own experiences, as well as countless other case studies and viewpoints from global experts in the native advertising field, on topics such as native content creation, programmatic native and measuring the success of your campaigns.

We'll also look at the native advertising mindset and what it takes to work as a native advertiser; and of course – what the future holds for native advertising.

There are some areas of native advertising that I have deliberately only touched upon in this book when it comes to offering how-to practical tips – for example, social media advertising. Why? There are literally hundreds of better books out there offering marketers superior, hands-on, practical advice on social media execution than I could ever do in these pages. So I make no apology for these very deliberate omissions.

But if you want to understand in more detail the native advertising ecosystem and how it is evolving, while picking up some good practical advice along the way, this book is for you. In fact, at the time of writing it's the only book in existence that covers this topic in any level of detail.

I've deliberately included many personal stories and experiences in this book, because we all love stories. And stories sit at the heart of native advertising.

By the time you are finished reading this book, you will hopefully know all you need to know about native advertising. But also, I hope you will know a lot more about the wider digital world, especially the business side of digital. It's an ambitious aim for a book that, when I started, I thought would be very niche in scope.

Native advertising will continue to influence and affect our daily lives for many years to come. This book is my attempt to highlight the creative, technological and commercial aspects at play behind these ads. I hope you enjoy it.

Why native advertising matters

Digital advertising is a world built on buzzwords, acronyms and expectation. Each year there's a new phrase that is de rigueur and that promises to answer all our digital ad problems. For veterans in the space – and confused marketers trying to understand what's important and what's not – it's all too easy to become confused, cynical, and even a little hostile, to the launch of ever more buzzwords.

If you fall into this bracket, this chapter is for you. In this chapter I aim to show why native advertising is more than just another buzzword.

The rise of content marketing

Today we live in a digital landscape where content is everywhere. You are nothing online if you do not create content. As I wrote in the chapter on 'Content marketing and native advertising' in Damian Ryan's *Understanding Digital Marketing*, 'content in its myriad different forms is the currency that digital marketers use to engage, interact with and influence their customers'.[1]

If you are looking for a longer synopsis on content marketing and how it fits into digital marketing as a whole, I recommend you start with Ryan's book. But in summary, the proliferation of content creation by brands is a key driver behind native advertising.

More and more brands are creating their own content. Brands such as General Electric (GE), for example, continue to invest heavily in content marketing. Coca-Cola – one of the biggest brands on the planet – has put content at the core of its 'Content 2020' advertising strategy mission, which perhaps sums up why there is more and more branded content being created across the board:

All advertisers need a lot more content so that they can keep the engagement with consumers fresh and relevant, because of the 24/7 connectivity. If you're going to be successful around the world, you have to have fat and fertile ideas at the core.[2]

The barriers to entry for creating and publishing your own content, as a brand, are considerably lower than they were in the pre-digital age. The cost for a business to launch and run a blog is negligible, even for the smallest of companies; reaching an audience via social media and search engines is possible. Content marketing is not new. John Deere, the tractor maker, created and published its own magazine, *The Furrow*, as far back as 1895. Michelin, the tyre manufacturer, began producing a maintenance guide filled with travel and accommodation recommendations for French motorists in 1900; Nike published and promoted a 19-page booklet entitled *Jogging* in 1966, practically inventing the sport of running in the US in the process. But the scale of content creation – and the appetite of consumers for content in an always-on digital-first world – is new.

The content marketing myth

In some ways brands were duped with content. They were sold a falsehood. They were told by experts in search, social media and digital marketing that if they created content and published it on their blogs, they would be inundated with new leads, followers, likes and shares. All they needed to do was create content – and lots of it. So brands and agencies found themselves setting up content studios – or factories, depending on the business and your point of view – that pumped out reams and reams of content, of differing levels of quality. It was sometimes content for content's sake. It was too expensive, too complicated, too abstract and unquantifiable. There was little to justify content creation at a senior level. The C-suite didn't get it. Many brands retreated away from content as a result. It didn't work for them.

But somewhere in the jumble of content were some great ideas – and great stories – that audiences and customers clearly would love to discover. There was, in amongst the clutter, the personality behind the brands shining through. But no one could find it. No one knew it existed most of the time. Or rather, only very few people could find it. This is where native advertising came in.

Native advertising as content distributor

Native advertising rose as a way to distribute brand content to an audience. First, it developed on platforms such as Facebook, Twitter and LinkedIn, before moving to wider publisher environments. For those brands that did not create their own content, but rather used the services of publishers to create and host bespoke content for their brand, they now had a new term to describe what had once been known as advertorials – but with wider reach, more creativity and far better measurement criteria thrown into the mix too.

Native advertising offered a way for brands to promote the content they were creating. It added a paid-for element to the 'earned' media that content marketing offered them. Native advertising allows a business to grow content marketing efforts. It allows content to scale.

In summary   Content is key to digital advertising today. Native advertising is the default distribution model for this branded content.

A mobile-first world

The consumer appetite for content – be it brand content or standard editorial – is driven by mobile. We live in a mobile-first world dominated by feeds. The average person has upwards of 76 sessions with their phone per day. Power users average 132 phone sessions per day. Research carried out by dscout, a mobile research platform that collects and analyses video, image, text and survey feedback for businesses, found that while sessions with our phones can be broken down into the above number, we do in fact touch, tap and swipe our phones a total of 2,617 times a day on average. It's a big number. Daily, the average smartphone user interacts with their devices for a total of 145 minutes, or 2 hours 25 minutes. Heavier users: 225 daily minutes, or 3 hours 45 minutes.[3]

On desktop, the feed remains powerful. Countless heat map studies that follow eye movement across a page show that the feed is where our attention lies. Areas to the right of the content on the page – where traditionally publishers run banner advertising – are ignored.

The importance of feeds

For a large proportion of people interacting with their phones at this time, they do so looking to consume content distributed via a feed. Facebook feeds, Instagram feeds, Pinterest feeds, Twitter feeds, app feeds, publisher feeds: the feed is where your customers congregate, day in, day out.

The feed is the TV set at home and the water-cooler at work of modern marketing. And the only way to gain your customer's attention in-feed is through content. Aggressive promotions do not work: at best they are ignored; at worst they spark an online backlash few businesses are equipped to handle. Interruptions are seldom rewarded unless they offer entertaining or informative content. If not, your customers have moved on in the feed.

A 2015 study found that the average online user had an attention span of just 8 seconds, down from 12 seconds in 2000. So you can see the problem you have to engage on mobile.[4]

Interesting content is the only way to interact with your audience across the feed. Native advertising formats are the only way to successfully deliver this content and get any sort of engagement.

The power of stories

Digital advertising offers a lot of promise. It promises scale on a level few other advertising mediums can possibly imagine. If you want to run an ad campaign targeting Indian teenagers, and a simultaneous campaign targeting Australian grandmothers, you can do this far, far more easily digitally than with other ad formats. It promises accountability that is unparalleled: advertisers can and do track their ad spend – and the reach this spend generates – down to the very last cent. Advertisers can attribute and measure a return on all activity they run. They know which activity generates the most sales, for example. A popular digital advertising mantra is: 'Right person, right time, right place.'

Sophisticated ad technology means that this mantra is a reality for many digital advertisers today. The promise is that no advertising spend is wasted on the wrong type of targeting; the return on investment is strong. In the majority of cases, digital advertising delivers on these promises.

When faced with endless technological changes promising more and more data, targeting and measureable performance, many digital marketers forgot some of the core tenets of effective advertising – to tell a story. Instead, particularly in the early days of digital, online ads often resembled boring matter-of-fact product information listings and stale banner boxes. They did nothing for the imagination. But it didn't matter, apparently, because everything could be tracked and analysed and a return on investment counted. Advertisers were happy.

As digital has evolved, the novelty of being online for most consumers has disappeared – and with it the novelty of clicking on banner ads – as consumers and technology become more advanced, those practices no longer work.

Legendary ad man David Ogilvy is famous for saying, 'You cannot bore people into buying your product; you can only interest them in buying it.'[5] How do you interest people in a product or service? Make it personal to them. And one of the best ways to do this is to tell them a story.

This is not just marketing speak, either; there is a growing body of evidence highlighting the importance that stories play in how our brains store memories and organize information.

Storytelling and memory

We all love stories. But few people had realized quite how important stories and storytelling are to our development until just recently.

As a species we immerse ourselves in stories. It's to do with how we process information. In fact, anthropologists, scientists and historians believe that it is the unique human ability to tell and share stories that has been fundamental to our success as a species. Yuval Noah Harari, in his bestseller *Sapiens: A brief history of humankind*, argues that it is our ability to understand stories – or 'fictions' – collectively that propelled *Homo sapiens* on the road from hunter-gatherers to the dominant global species we are today: 'Fiction has enabled us not merely to imagine things, but to do so *collectively*.'[6]

Stories have always been at the heart of our species. We collectively use them to imagine our own and others' futures, and to work towards collective goals with other people. Stories are the vehicles we use to get our thoughts across to others – and to convince one another that a specific course of action is the correct one to take.

But we are also hardwired as individuals to think in a narrative fashion. We use stories to make decisions and to remember things.

In January 2016, Jonas Kaplan of the University of Southern California revealed how real-time brain scans show that stories that force us to think about our deepest values activate a region of the brain once thought to be its autopilot.[7] 'Stories appear to be a fundamental way in which the brain organizes information in a practical and memorable manner,' says Kaplan.

In most people a story will always engender some sort of emotional response – be it love, laughter, fear, anger or even boredom. The story will create an emotional response. It's why all the very best advertising tells a story – and connects with you.

Very few things can do this. In fact, without experiencing something yourself, almost nothing else can. A story is what makes us human. Stories are what triggers our imagination. To enjoy a story you need to: 1) picture yourself in the story, imagine ourselves to be in a certain place or experience; and 2) have some emotional empathy to the participants of the said story.

These are fundamental human traits: imagination, empathy, desire. Smell is often associated with memory and emotions; but what does it actually trigger? More often than not, a certain smell will trigger a memory, which then triggers a certain story in your head. For example, the smell of fresh cut grass may trigger a memory in many people of summer days from their childhood, playing in the garden; while for others it may remind them of playing sport – football or tennis – and the story of a particularly great game they played.

Memories are stories, and stories are simply ways of accessing stored emotions. Where there is human emotion, there is always a story.

'When people read stories we invoke personal experiences. We're relying not just on words on a page, but also our own past experiences,' says Raymond Mar, Associate Psychology Professor at York University, Toronto, and author of a study published in 2014 on fiction and its relation to real-world empathy, cognition and behaviour. 'We often have thoughts and emotions that are consistent with what's going on in a story. Even though fiction is fabricated, it can communicate truths about human psychology and relationships.'[8]

How we build our personal stories day to day

Every minute of every day we are writing our own narratives in our heads, consciously and subconsciously. For every posed selfie, Snapchat or Instagram of a meal we take – the conscious creation of a very public personal narrative we want to show to the world – there are 10, 20 or 30 subliminal stories taking place in our day-to-day lives.

We just don't recognize them often. What goes on your feed is the self-edited, copy-reviewed story we like to project to the world. But every minute of every day we are living out our narratives – and whether we know it or not, every decision we make is in part our decision to 'tell' the story of our lives. We are always planning for the future or analysing a past event – and we imagine all of this via storytelling. This is why, as a species, we like stories so much – and why marketers have always tried to convey their messages via stories.

What do stories have to do with native advertising?

So some readers may be thinking – all very interesting, but what does this have to do with native advertising? Well, it has a lot to do with it. Stories are at the heart of all the very best content marketing activity – and native advertising works best when it is promoting the very best stories.

How do we decide whether an idea or course of action is any good? How do we decide whether or not to buy that product or service? Why do we decide to book with that business, over another? We use our imaginations to create a story of the what, how, when nature of the problem that the idea is perceived to solve and imagine us 'winning' the story.

It's the same process your customers go through when you present your advertising messages to them. The story it imparts and the emotions it triggers are immediate. Are you telling a good story with your advertising messages? Have you triggered the response you want – and need to achieve – for them to interact with your brand?

The modern-day collective campfire

If we look back to pre-history to a time when we used to collectively gather around the campfire and share stories, our biology and cognitive make-up has changed very little. Now fast forward to the present day – we are still looking for stories and open to sharing them. But nowadays, instead of the campfire, where are we congregating?

Increasingly as a collective we are congregating around the 'feed' on our mobile devices – social media feeds such as Facebook, Twitter, Instagram, LinkedIn and more, as well as myriad different publisher feeds and apps. Every time we check into the feed, we are consciously – but also subconsciously, to a certain extent – looking for a story fix. We are looking for a collective story to talk with others about and share.

Native advertising allows brands to bring their stories to the modern-day 'collective campfire'. It plugs directly into one of our core human characteristics – our insatiable need for stories.

The best advertising always has story appeal

None of this is new to non-digital advertisers – Ogilvy, for example, knew all of this when he worked in the *Mad Men* era of the 1950s and 1960s. But it is relatively new to some digital marketers. When content marketing grew in significance in the late 2000s, it finally put the content – or the story – of the marketing messages back on the digital agenda. Before then, it was certainly overlooked.

Native advertising helps place creativity back on the digital agenda

As a performance-driven medium, the first 20+ years of digital advertising have been mostly about return on investment for advertisers. What can we do for better advertiser performance? How can we squeeze more value for the brand? Performance metrics – clicks, impressions, dwell times, shares, leads, sales – are the criteria for success or failure. This is no bad thing; after all, better returns are what have helped grow the digital advertising market to what it is today – a multi-billion-dollar-a-year industry.

But the story has been overlooked. Creativity has generally come in second place to performance. The value exchange and narrative story between the consumer and the advertising formats themselves were never, or only lightly, considered, and got lost somewhere in the blur of intrusive ad formats, performance indicators and analytic metrics. This is important to note.

There has been an over-reliance on behavioural metrics such as clicks, visits and interactions. 'These provide a narrow view of online and mobile as purely behavioural response channels. This overlooks the full potential of these platforms as brand building and demand-driving communications channels,' wrote James Galpin, Head of Media and Digital LATAM at Millward Brown, a leading market research and advertising effectiveness company, in their *Digital & Media Predictions 2016* report.[9]

But this is beginning to change. And it will continue to change as the rise of native advertising continues. The corresponding decline in banner advertising performance and the increased prevalence of content marketing and native advertising distribution formats has led to a long overdue re-evaluation of the digital value exchange, and story-based marketing is very much at the forefront of this change.

Technology and creativity combine

While native advertising may have been born as the natural advertising medium for content distribution and a mobile-first world, another key reason behind the growth of native advertising concerns technology and creativity. Art and science are now combined. The convergence of cutting-edge technology and creativity to offer story-led advertising opportunities means that what can or cannot be done when it comes to digital advertising is largely limited only to our imaginations. As an ad medium, native advertising gives you far more room to flex your creative muscles. The technology is there to help, not hinder you.

We will cover in more detail digital advertising methods around data, retargeting and programmatic native advertising in later chapters, but from a purely technological point of view, native advertising has many advantages. It's very hard to engage with an audience in a small banner ad, especially one that is pushed out into the periphery and ignored. It's basically a box. You can fill it with text or an image, or both. That's about it.

Native advertising formats offer more alternatives. If the idea works, you can make it happen.

You can lead with content teasers that then click through to larger, more in-depth pieces of editorial content that offer true immersive experiences. Or you can create interactive elements that generate quantifiable return on investment, or you can blend video with content, embed social media, quizzes and much, much more.

In short, whatever a publisher does on the editorial side of things, you can do from a technical point of view with native advertising.

Video advertising

Marketers know that video is increasingly the key to building brand in digital. Video is a powerful marketing tool and one of the most successful forms of content that a brand can produce for digital in terms of engagement, shares, likes and interaction. It's growing all the time. And in-feed video formats are increasingly becoming the most popular video format that advertisers look to use.

Native advertising formats work equally well for video as they do for other forms of content. This is a major plus point for native advertising when the uptake in video ads – and the distribution of those videos at scale – is increasingly high on an advertiser's agenda. Like mobile browsing and content marketing, video advertising is also here to stay, which augers well for native advertising market growth.

Display advertising and programmatic

The traditional digital display advertising market is predicted to shrink in the future, albeit from a relatively high starting point. More and more digital advertising budgets – budgets that advertisers apportion to running banner ads – are moving into native advertising. Why? Put simply, it's because the performance of native advertising far exceeds that of display advertising. Users see, engage, click and respond to native advertising. So when you compare like for like, there is no competition between display advertising and native advertising.

Until 2015, though, the buying model for native advertising was very different. Trading of display advertising is now largely done programmatically (see Chapter 15 for a fuller explanation), whereas until 2015, trading native advertising programmatically was limited. This has changed as technology, the market demand and platforms have advanced, so much so that now it is incredibly straightforward to buy and run programmatic native advertising campaigns. There is much more on this in the programmatic native chapter, of course. But this change is one of the key drivers in advertising buying habits that means native advertising as a medium is set to grow in the future.

Ad blocking

Ad blockers, as the name suggests, is a type of software you can run on your computer or mobile device that removes advertising from publisher websites. It is a growing problem for publishers and the advertising world. In the UK, it is estimated that around 9.2 million of the UK adults who regularly use the internet do so while running ad blocking. Research published by the Internet Advertising Bureau (IAB) in July 2016 claimed that 26 per cent of all desktop users and 15 per cent of mobile consumers use ad blockers.[10] In the US, eMarketer reported that 69.8 million Americans were estimated to use an ad blocker in 2016, a jump of 34.4 per cent from 2015. In 2017 this figure is estimated to grow an additional 24 per cent to include 86.6 million people.[11]

These are staggering numbers. While it may mean that consumers get to visit websites without any interruption from advertising messages, it leaves publishers – many of whom are already struggling to cope with dwindling print revenue – with no way of monetizing the people that are visiting their websites and consuming their content for free. Advertisers meanwhile cannot reach digitally large swathes of their target audience.

Ad blocking is a crisis verging on a catastrophe for the industry. There is continued debate on the topic. Publishers are experimenting with different approaches.

In some markets, publishers have taken an aggressive stance on ad-block users. Germany is one country where large publishing groups – combined with less international competition for content created in German, so users have fewer alternatives when looking to consume relevant content – may have been able to have an impact. It is estimated that around 25 per cent of Germans use an ad blocker.

German publisher Bild has a tough position on ad blockers, banning users who have the software enabled when they visit their publications. Smaller publishers do the same. Multiple others, such as Gruner + Jahr, ask users to disable their ad blockers while visiting their sites.

It is an approach that may be making some impact. The German digital media trade body Bundesverband Digitale Wirtschaft claimed in November 2016 that ad-block usage may have peaked.[12] But only time will tell.

In other markets throughout the world, publishers and advertisers are running similar activity. Pay walls and subscription services are being trialled and different models experimented with. The results differ from publisher to publisher, country to country. There's no one-size-fits-all approach to winning.

Ad blocking, acceptable ads and the business side of ad blocking software

Contributed by Jamie Toward, Managing Partner, Content, Karmarama

Ah… ad blocking, what an interesting conundrum you are. From a consumer point of view, ad blocking is a genuine boon. Page load speeds increase, data allocations on mobile tariffs go further and, of course, those pesky ads aren't landing in feeds any more.

Let's rewind a little and work out how we got to the point where over 100 million devices (yep, that's eight zeros) use ad-block software…

The motivations for consumers to install ad blockers are manifold and intertwined. However, most studies agree that the top five motivations are:

- security – malware protection;
- interruption – ads aggressively interceding in a content consumption moment (reading or viewing, basically);
- speed – slow website loading times (coupled with, in some studies, the consumption of data tariff on mobile contracts);
- too many ads – simply too many ad units running on pages;
- privacy – third-party tracking.

These are all entirely reasonable reasons for anybody to install an ad blocker. However, it's interesting to couple these views with an insight from some IAB 2016 research. Over half of the people who've installed ad blockers don't realize that running an ad blocker restricts revenue to the publisher and the subsequent knock-on effect on job security in the publishing sector.

So consumers, while a little ill-informed about the consequences of running an ad blocker, are doing what consumers have always done – look for ways to enjoy their media consumption in peace. Let's be clear: people have done this since media started using ad-funded business models. People flip past ad pages in magazines, only read the editorial in broadsheets, fast forward TVCs on their personal video recorder, get to the cinema after the trailers and, of course, that typically British trait of nipping off to make a cup of tea while the ads are on. Nothing new here then?

Well, yes, this time there is. All those other instances of ad avoidance are facilitated by the consumer. They are physically choosing, by themselves, to avoid those ad moments. But in their digital worlds, they're receiving help from the ad-block manufacturers. And that's where things start to get a bit murky.

The ad-block manufacturers need to make money out of their business. That's right and proper, and organizations should get a return on their labour and investment.

The real murky part is in *how* the manufacturers make money. Most ad-block provider business models are predicated on a (relatively) small fee to the consumer for downloading the software. But some, most notably the largest ad-block provider in the world, Eyeo (manufacturer of AdBlock Plus or ABP), also generate revenue from publishers.

Large publishers can pay to ensure their ads are whitelisted (permitted for display through AdBlock Plus). Ostensibly this payment is used to fund the development of 'acceptable ads'. 'Acceptable ads' for Eyeo are ads that carry little weight (the amount of data required to render the ad), have limited tracking and specifically are non-intrusive. These ads are permitted via ABP for any publisher, for any advertiser, as they are deemed to not interfere unnecessarily with the user experience.

But this approach to generating revenue raises questions immediately:

1 When and how did Eyeo come to be the representative of consumers?

2 Can any commercial organization claim to transparently represent 'the view of all consumers'?

3 Should Eyeo alone set the rules of what is deemed to be 'acceptable' in digital advertising?

4 Are all the revenues provided by 'large publishers' used exclusively for the 'acceptable advertising' initiative, or do those revenues 'leak' into other parts of Eyeo?

5 What is a 'Large Publisher' and how is it defined?

Ultimately it must be recognized that Eyeo is not a not-for-profit organization and, as soon as it took money to allow ads through AdBlock Plus, the moral position of providing a public good to combat poor advertising behaviour (through negligence or otherwise) was compromised.

Paid whitelists smack of Eyeo running a business model that will cause difficulties for other businesses unless those businesses can pay Eyeo to collaborate with them – and that sounds very much like a protection racket.

The controversy around AdBlock Plus increased in the third quarter of 2016 when it announced the launch of an 'acceptable ad exchange'. Effectively, this was the proposed launch of a trading platform for those ads that Eyeo can run without intruding upon the consumer's media consumption experience.

This really was an extraordinary move by AdBlock Plus that seemed to show they had no compunction about extending their questionable business practices into the very programmatic trading environment that facilitates some of the user issues that they purportedly seek to solve – perhaps the greatest move of 'poacher turned gamekeeper' that the media industry has ever seen.

Rightly, scorn poured from all sides and AppNexus and Google (between them handling much of the 'plumbing' that delivers programmatic trading) refused to cooperate with the initiative. To date (March 2017), the 'acceptable ad exchange' has not re-emerged from the wreckage of its initial launch and the entire industry should hope that AdBlock Plus initiatives in this area are discontinued permanently.

The heart of Eyeo's business may be sound. After all, helping consumers do something they've done for years in other media is sound – especially if it's helping address real consumer concerns about security, privacy and speed. But if Eyeo is prepared to take money from elements of the advertising 'system', it should not just be focusing on investing that money in identifying 'acceptable ads'. It should also be focusing on spending some of that money in communicating with consumers that 'free' content is not really 'free'. It costs money to make and many people have jobs that are dependent upon the ad-funded model. If they want to help the world produce better advertising and help consumers have better digital experiences, they also have an obligation to educate those very consumers as to the implications of running AdBlock Plus. And taking that action might make Eyeo seem more like the business with a social conscience it claims to be.

You can't claim to want to 'make the internet better for everyone' (Eyeo's words) without also explaining how the internet works to everyone – then users can 'decide how the internet runs' (again Eyeo's words) with real clarity. At the minute, it feels like Eyeo is deciding how the internet runs and is feathering their nest with a questionable business model while they're doing it.

What does this have to do with native advertising?

Consumers want better ads. The main reason millions of people go to the effort of downloading ad blockers is not really down to the fact that they have a pathological hatred of advertising. It's just that the advertising they have been exposed to online is infuriating and overly interruptive: video ads that start immediately blasting out at high volume as soon as a page loads; full page pop-ups that you can't seem to close; sites so crowded with advertising that they take what feels like 15 years to load – and they constantly interrupt the user experience throughout. The digital industry is all too guilty of these things. In the race to monetize digital publications, the user experience went out of the window. Ad blocking is a consumer reaction to this.

As an industry, advertisers and publishers have had to sit up and take notice. Native advertising is part of the response to this. Many publishers see it as the solution to ad blocking. Certain forms of branded content publisher partnership native advertising – when run through the content management systems of publications – are harder, but not impossible, to block by ad blockers; for example, other forms of native advertising that integrate into a publication via JavaScript code can be blocked more easily by ad blockers.

Native advertising reduces the need for ad blockers

Native advertising is not a technical solution to the technicalities of ad blockers. But it is a format that could help reduce the desire to install an ad blocker in the first place. Why? Native advertising formats are less intrusive. They do not take over the pages of websites – they sit within the look and feel of a publication; and as a consumer you choose to interact with them. The challenge for advertisers is to take away the desire for consumers to want to use ad blockers. So how exactly do we do that?

Be less annoying. Native ads are less annoying than most other digital advertising formats. Ad blocking has been a wake-up call to the digital advertising world. It's a challenge, but it's also an opportunity. It's an opportunity to take digital advertising to the next level using better advertising formats, technology and the tools already at our disposal.

Native advertising is part of the change in what consumers deem acceptable advertiser behaviour in the digital space. It's about maintaining the correct balance between advertiser and consumer; it's about maintaining the value exchange.

Millennials and the value exchange

The value exchange is discussed a lot in advertising circles – and you can hardly go a day in digital marketing without mention of Millennials, too. Both play a key part in explaining why and how native advertising has risen in popularity.

But before we start, let's get the definitions out of the way.

The definition of the value exchange

In its simplest form, the value exchange is this: both the brand and the consumer need to get something out of the advertising message exchange or interaction. There has to be some value in it for both parties. Advertisers see the value in having an opportunity to promote their products to customers; but it's also important that customers see some value in the advertising messages put in front of them. To be successful, advertisers have to offer something of interest, or something that entertains consumers. Think of every TV ad you've ever seen that made you laugh: the value exchange there is that the advertiser has entertained you, in exchange for the opportunity to promote to you. Got it? Right, let's move on.

The definition of a Millennial

A Millennial is a person that theoretically reached young adulthood at the turn of the millennium and early 21st century. But the reality, depending on which marketing research paper, title or newspaper you read, lumps Millennials into those born anywhere between 1980 and 2000, or 1984 and 2000, or for some it's 1982 to 2002. It can be confusing, but hopefully you get the picture.

The value exchange in digital advertising

Traditionally, marketing messages have been delivered to captive audiences – TV, print, radio, cinema – where there is very little perceived value exchange. In these scenarios, consumers are at the mercy of what the advertiser wants them to see. It's a one-way street.

Millennials don't work like that. They expect the value exchange to be present. Their time is precious. In exchange for their time interacting with your brand, they expect something in return. They expect a brand to entertain them. Or to offer them information they find interesting. This doesn't mean that Millennials hate advertising.

Provided that the 'value exchange' is there, Millennials are happy to engage. An ADYOULIKE study of 1,000 UK adults aged 18–33 in 2015 found that over half of UK Millennials (57 per cent) will happily visit online content that appeals to them, even if it has been obviously paid for or sponsored.[13]

Millennials do not expect a brand to hammer them with the hard sell, or – even worse – boring ads filled with irrelevant messaging, delivered in formats that are intrusive and annoying. That's never been cool, but it really isn't any more. It's digital brand suicide.

All demographic groups are changing their behaviour towards advertising. But whether you are a Millennial or not, it's worth noting that we've all changed how we use technology, consume media and engage with advertisers. It's just that the younger generation act this way en masse, and have been 'early adopters' of this new viewpoint.

Baby Boomers are more fickle in their media consumption than they were 10 or 15 years ago, for example, because, well, they can be: like the rest of us, they have far more options and demands on their precious time than they did a generation ago.

A Nielsen study published in March 2015 found that 25 per cent of Baby Boomers regularly watch video programming on a mobile device, and over half of Baby Boomer respondents said they use electronic devices to listen to music and take or share photos.[14]

All age groups (apart from perhaps the very old) use social media; they multi-screen; they watch videos on YouTube; they skip ads – who would have thought it? – just like Millennials.

The problem with Millennial and demographic groupings

Millennials, if you didn't already know, are big news in marketing. As a demographic, Millennials are numerous – and have unique advertising spending power. The purchasing power of Millennials is estimated to be $170 billion per year, according to ComScore research published in 2012. There are approximately 79 million Millennials in the US, far more than the 48 million Generation Xers (born between 1965 and 1980). Millennials are the largest generation since the Baby Boomers (born between 1946 and 1964).[15]

But lumping entire generations into 20-year blocks has its challenges. With such a disparate demographic, it's obvious to see that Millennials are not a homogenous mass of similar tastes, views and actions. If you take this broad definition of Millennial as starting from 1980 onwards, I'm a Millennial, just: I was born in 1980. But my 20-year-old student nephew is certainly a Millennial, too. We sit pretty much at either end of the Millennial age range. And our lives are completely different.

I'm a daily commuter, run a business, have a mortgage, a wife and young child. I have early nights, grocery deliveries and weekend trips to the park. He has all-day drinking sessions, exams, girlfriends, all-night parties, and, to my ongoing envy, lie-ins!

Joel Windels, VP, Inbound Marketing, at social media monitoring firm Brandwatch, writing in March 2016 for the Social Media Week website,[16] summed up the issue many marketers have with the term Millennial:

> But what does Millennial actually mean? We're talking about a twenty-year age range encompassing over 75 million Americans. In 2016, a Millennial could be anything from a 16-year-old schoolgirl still living with her parents, to a home-owning family man in his mid-30s.

David Measer, SVP and Group Strategic Planning Director for agency RPA, explained to Digiday in April 2016 that categorizing Millennials as one group was 'like saying everything living in the ocean is "fish". When we stereotype great numbers of people for the purpose of selling them stuff, it comes off as, well, condescending.'[17]

But while there are problems with lumping such a large, disparate age group together, there are certainly some traits Millennials share: importantly, for example, their ease with new technology and their digital habits. So whether you love, like or loathe the word, for the purposes of this section I refer to this age group as 'Millennials.' Sorry about that.

You no longer have a captive audience

Digital has changed the 'captive' audience forever. Even when we are watching TV, most of us are often 'second-screening' on our smartphones and tablets. Marketers need to 'earn' the right to advertise to everyone in this hyper-connected, always-on world, where content is currency and customer attention is easily lost at the swipe of a finger or click of a mouse.

It's not just Millennials. Whatever the demographic, consumers expect more from advertisers. As digital marketers, it's time that we all start to think this way for every demographic and every campaign, not just for those buzzwordy, hard-to-define Millennial-types.

CASE STUDY Native distribution: Microsoft

Microsoft were looking to generate increased awareness among students during the back to school season in the US for digital note-taking app OneNote. Microsoft face ongoing competition with Apple and were keen to reach students, whose buying decisions often follow them throughout their lives. Targeting Millennial students to drive OneNote usage was key.

Microsoft partnered with native advertising platform Sharethrough. OneNote opted to use Sharethrough's content engagement ads to amplify six Tumblr posts, which included a long-form Robert Downey Jr video and a Vine video created with Vine influencer Zach King. These ad units take existing brand content and fit natively across publisher pages.

Results

- 15 million viewable impressions;
- +52% engagement rate compared with pre-card campaigns;
- +58% creative optimization.

Why it worked

Relevant, high-quality content created for the Tumblr environment was used to extend the OneNote reach to relevant Millennial audiences. Within the card, the Tumblr post appeared with social sharing buttons and unique calls to action, as well as the Tumblr follow button, which allowed for additional 'earned media' reach when the content shared. Content cards, keeping users onsite, offered a 52% increase in performance compared with clicking out; while creative optimizations around headlines and thumbnails, which delivered a 58% increase in performance, also assisted in making the campaign a success.[18]

Find out more at: www.sharethrough.com/advertisers/microsoft/

Native advertising: caught by the buzz?

In this chapter we've looked at some of the fundamental trends in digital advertising today, and how consumer behaviour is leading to greater adoption of different ad formats and ways of reaching consumers with digital messaging. The ongoing interest in brand content, exciting ad formats and the combination of emerging technology and creativity mean that native advertising is well placed to grow exponentially in the years ahead. In the next few chapters we'll go deeper, showcasing why it is so powerful.

Interview with Jesper Laursen, CEO, Native Advertising Institute

How would you describe native advertising in one sentence? Do you think there's confusion around what it is?

Native advertising is paid media where the unit matches the form, feel, function and quality of the content of the media on which it appears.

And yes, there is a lot of confusion. But native advertising is the umbrella under which you can put sponsored content (long form), paid social, programmatic, certain paid e-mail marketing, and influencer advertising, to mention some of the most important ones. Some mistake these for being something different from native advertising.

Why do you think it has become so successful?

First of all, consumers have become fed up with the mid to bottom-funnel, brand-centric advertising that they have endured for years. They are so tired of brands talking about themselves and their products instead of addressing the pain points, problems, dreams and aspirations of their consumers.

One reason we know this to be true is the rapid rise of ad blocking. It's essentially consumers sending a clear message to advertisers telling them that they have had enough. The customers have taken control and they decide who can talk to them, what you can talk to them about and when. And if you want to have their attention, you need to start talking about something that they find interesting. They no longer accept being interrupted when they spend time on a media platform. If they are there to be informed, inspired or entertained, that is what you as a brand should do.

Native is at the heart of the business model of social media platforms such as Facebook. They have effectively killed organic reach, so if you want to talk to their audience, you have to pay to gain access to users' newsfeeds.

Finally, paid distribution has become an inevitable part of content marketing. The old content credo 'if you build it, they will come' doesn't work any more because the search engines have become saturated with content and the lack of organic reach on social media. If you want to get your content in front of an audience and drive traffic, you need to pay to play.

What is the number one question you get asked about native advertising?

'How do you make native advertising that actually drives tangible business results?'

Do you think the acceptance of and view of native advertising is the same in every country? Which countries get it?

The US and the UK have traditionally been more advanced when it comes to native advertising. But really it is much more down to individual players than markets. We host the Native Advertising Awards and we see really amazing work from small countries such as Croatia, so it mostly comes down to one brilliant publisher, for example. On the other hand, we see terrible work by big agencies or publishers in mature markets, so it's hard to point to specific countries that get it.

How does native advertising differ from content marketing?
Are the two aligned?

It is our belief that native advertising will be part of most content marketing projects in the near future, so there will continue to be some confusion between the two. But a rule of thumb is that content marketing has owned media at heart and, for the most part, gets distributed on earned or paid channels. Native advertising always takes place on somebody else's platform. A brand can run a blog and it will be content marketing, but when they take some of that content and run a paid campaign on LinkedIn, the resulting native advertising is the distribution of the content marketing output – owned media. Content studios (internal agencies at publications) don't necessarily see it that way. Marketers or journalists at a content studio are essentially doing content marketing (producing owned media) and publishing it on the publication they work for. However, for the brand that's paying for the content and controlling some of the editorial, it's most certainly native advertising. This is where a lot of the confusion lies.

What do you see as the future of native advertising?

Over the next few years we're going to see a very steep learning curve for everybody involved. Native has been around for decades, but the real evolution is happening right now, and with all the budgets and resources pouring into the space, magic is going to happen. This means better content, better strategies, better collaboration and better results.

Legacy publishers will also finally find a way for native to peacefully co-exist with their editorial content. Publishers will also play a very important part in the disruption that is happening in the agency world because they are much better equipped for executing on this than traditional agencies.

The Native Advertising Institute is dedicated to helping marketers become successful with native advertising. It is a great resource of information and thought leadership on the topic of native advertising. Find out more at: www.nativeadvertisinginstitute.com

Endnotes

1   Ryan, D (2016) *Understanding Digital Marketing*, Kogan Page, London

2   Pulizzi, J (4 January 2012) Coca-Cola bets the farm on content marketing: Content 2020 [online] http://contentmarketinginstitute.com/2012/01/coca-cola-content-marketing-20-20/ [accessed 27 March 2017]

3   Winnick, M (16 June 2016) Putting a finger on our phone obsession [online] https://blog.dscout.com/mobile-touches [accessed 27 March 2017]

4   Watson, L (15 May 2015) Humans have shorter attention span than goldfish thanks to smartphones [online] www.telegraph.co.uk/science/2016/03/12/humans-have-shorter-attention-span-than-goldfish-thanks-to-smart/ [accessed 27 March 2017]

5   Ogilvy & Mather (no date) Corporate Culture: What we believe and how we behave [online] www.ogilvy.com/About/Our-History/Corporate-Culture.aspx [accessed 27 March 2017]

6   Harari, YN (2015) *Sapiens: A brief history of humankind*, Vintage, London

7   University of Southern California (7 January 2016) Zoning out or deep thinking? [online] www.eurekalert.org/pub_releases/2016-01/uosc-zoo010616.php [accessed 27 March 2017]

8   Society for Personality and Social Psychology (11 August 2014) Can fiction stories make us more empathetic? [online] https://www.sciencedaily.com/releases/2014/08/140811151632.htm [accessed 27 March 2017]

9   Millward Brown (no date) Digital & Media Predictions 2016 [online] www.millwardbrown.com/mb-global/our-thinking/insights-opinion/articles/digital-predictions/2016/2016-digital-and-media-predictions#download [accessed 27 March 2017]

10   Johnson, L (26 July 2016) IAB study says 26% of desktop users turn on ad blockers [online] www.adweek.com/digital/iab-study-says-26-desktop-users-turn-ad-blockers-172665/ [accessed 27 March 2017]

11   eMarketer (21 June 2016) US ad blocking to jump by double digits this year [online] www.emarketer.com/Article/US-Ad-Blocking-Jump-by-Double-Digits-This-Year/1014111 [accessed 27 March 2017]

12   Bi Intelligence (29 November 2016) Ad blocking is declining in Germany [online] http://uk.businessinsider.com/german-ad-blocking-declines-2016-11?r=US&IR=T [accessed 27 March 2017]

13   Mortimer, N (15 March 2015) Six out of Ten Millenials Will Engage with Native Ads When Content Appeals [online] www.thedrum.com/news/2015/03/15/six-out-ten-millenials-will-engage-native-ads-when-content-appeals-0 [accessed 27 March 2017]

14   Nielsen (2015) Screen Wars: The battle for eye space in a TV-everywhere world [online] www.nielsen.com/content/dam/corporate/Italy/reports/2015/Nielsen%20Global%20Digital%20Landscape%20Report%20March%202015.pdf [accessed 27 March 2017]

15   ComScore (2012) Next-generation strategies for advertising to Millennials [online] www.comscore.com/Request/Presentations/2012/Millenials-Report-Download-January-2012?c=1] [accessed 27 March 2017]

16   Windels, J (24 March 2016) Millenials and marketing: Why brands are getting it so, so wrong [online] https://socialmediaweek.org/blog/2016/03/millennials-marketing-why-brands-are-getting-it-so-so-wrong/ [accessed 27 March 2017]

17 Chen, Y (6 April 2016) 'It's like saying everything living in the ocean is a fish': Marketers obsessed with millennials are making a mistake [online] http://digiday.com/marketing/advertisers-cool-millennial-talk/ [accessed 27 March 2017]

18 Sharethrough (no date) Microsoft used content engagement ads to reach Millennials for OneNote's Collective Project [online] https://sharethrough.app.box.com/s/nymu6jx20lzl58emymnwjzyfwvuetxgo and [accessed 27 March 2017]

A brief history of native advertising 04

Sponsored content is almost as old as publishing itself. In this chapter we aim to take you through a very brief history of the relationship advertising has always had with publishing. The aim is to show you how native advertising is very much just a part of this ongoing relationship. Native advertising as a term may be new, but the concept of native advertising has been around for a very long time.

I want to show you that while the native advertising you consume on Facebook, Twitter or LinkedIn, or share from BuzzFeed, Quartz, the *Guardian* and other publications, may feel all shiny and new, its roots hark back to the very early days of print journalism.

The yin and yang of publishing

There is a certain amount of snobbery in publishing when it comes to advertising. The divide between advertising and editorial – the yin and yang of any publication – can spill over into a somewhat snooty view of all things ad related among certain publisher people. This spills over into viewpoints on native advertising, too.

Many critics hark back to a time when advertising 'knew its place' and it was all about the story. This viewpoint is a complete fallacy, of course. The number-one aim of most media publications is to make money. It has always been the case. Advertising only 'knows its place' when publications are making fistfuls of cash.

The newspapers of the mid-twentieth century were hugely profitable. They ran lots of advertisements, but because the readerships were so strong – and advertisers clamoured to be included within their pages – a formula, or 'rules' if you like, emerged about what and where advertising should sit. Over time these rules, in many people's eyes, became laws – laws of publishing that had to be abided by. But these laws are not sacrosanct. And they stood in place for a relatively short period of time. What stood as a rule in 1980 was certainly not the rule in 1880.

Did you know, for example, that the vast majority of nineteenth-century newspapers, including *The Times*, ran their front covers with only advertising? In fact, most newspapers did not publish any news at all until at least three or four pages in.

As Andrew Marr writes:

> As Victorian prosperity booms, the sheer quantity of adverts makes filling the rest of the paper with interesting news harder and harder.[1]

The detailed, dull reports of parliamentary debates, long editorial op-ed pieces and moralizing, long-winded letters of correspondents from 'around the world', all of which came to characterize the content of late-Victorian newspapers, were a result of growing advertising demand. These Victorian versions of the rambling Facebook updates and Twitter rants we see today were editors' ways of increasing the content to run advertising against. The advertising came first, the content later. It was advertising that pushed forward the editorial agenda, helping launch new forms of journalism such as the columnist.

The majority of Victorian and early-twentieth-century newspapers carried sponsored content. Many included labels we'd be familiar with today. Take this example from the *Arizona Republican*, from Friday morning, 15 December 1911, which I quote in its entirety:

Advertisement for Arizona weather

Not a paid write-up, but a true story

Boys Find Ripe Melons on the Canal Bank and Go Swimming to Get Them
Here is a story filled full of meat for boosters, and garnished with all kinds of local colour: it also contains a moral, and is the best story that this writer has heard recently.

The members of a Phoenix family well known for their love of fine horseflesh and of God's good out of doors, were enjoying one of their accustomed rides, accompanied by some eastern friends. Their road led along the south side of the Arizona Canal about one-half miles from the cross-cut canal, when they noticed a boy, a horse and buggy standing by the side of rippling water, and almost simultaneously they caught

---

sight of the bared back of three small somethings, which for the sake of euphony and delicate sensibilities will be called Cupids. On the north bank of the canal just opposite the boy and the buggy, reposed three derelict watermelons, whose seeds had probably been carried there by picnickers, or deposited at flood time, which had taken root and had grown in fancied security in their unusual resting place.

It was away along at the last end of the fall, when the smell of Thanksgiving turkey fills the air and our eastern brothers are getting out their bob sleds, there these unconventional melons ripened and were spied by the Cupids and the properly clothed boy with the buggy. The sandias, as one's Mexican friends call them, were tempting, the water was warm and the boys were hungry; the result needs no description. The moral is that the home folks would have passed on their way, giving no thought to the affair, except to smile at the boys' fun, had it not been for their friends from the frozen states who thought that the fact of seeing lads eating watermelons while swimming in the latter part of November, to be exact, it was the 19th, was an event worthy of commemoration.[2]

This piece of commercial content was published over a hundred years ago. Yet there are some startling similarities between this piece and many pieces of native content we see today. The article, for example, appeared in-feed, surrounded by other short editorial stories. It was not, as latter publications did, sequestered to a peripheral news block.

The disclosure used is particularly of interest, too: 'Advertisement for Arizona weather.' There is full disclosure that this is an ad.

But the second part, 'Not a paid write-up, but a true story', is somewhat telling. If you glance through many old newspapers carefully you can see many instances of paid-for content. So much so in fact it could be argued that this second sub-title is included as a way of trying to legitimize the story in the eyes of a readership that was already familiar with paid-for content as a concept, and didn't expect what they were about to read to be true.

Those nostalgic about newspapers will also note this ad appeared in the 'morning edition', so there was almost certainly at least one more issue published of this paper each day.

While we are looking at this particular story, it's worth highlighting some additional key points around it. The title, although fairly tame by modern standards, does have many key elements of a good native headline. It is not salesy. It conveys meaning. This headline is in no way terrible – and is undoubtedly better than many modern-day examples of poor native headline generation.

It's also worth noting the emphasis on story. Whether true or not, it's interesting to note that over a hundred years ago savvy marketers knew that the best way to promote something that would resonate with a readership was through a story. Understanding who exactly placed this ad – and their exact motive – has eluded me in my research. At the time of publication, Arizona had just elected a new governor, and was just two months away from being admitted to the United States as the 48th state. So political reasoning may well have played a part. Whatever the reason, it's obvious those who paid for the ad wanted to highlight the exceptional Arizona weather, the potential of the farm land (watermelons just growing by themselves) and contrast it significantly with the 'frozen states' by highlighting the wintry conditions endured 'back east'. In a few sentences the writer does all of these things.

Interestingly, 103 years after the publication of this native ad, the Arizona Office of Tourism was still keen to attract those 'back east' – it launched a two-month, $200,000 winter advertising blitz in Chicago in 2014, reminding residents they could 'warm up in AZ'.[3]

Advertorials

As the print industry developed – and began to reach its zenith as the twentieth century unfolded – phrases such as 'advertorial' became commonly used to distinguish between what was commercial content and editorial. Advertorials were extremely common. They ranged from the blatant, to the subtler, sell. But in an age where it was impossible to research a topic at the click of a button, or flick of a thumb, advertorials certainly played a part in educating consumers. Without doubt, there was a brand message behind all of these advertorials, but they also imparted some interesting information. No publication was interested in writing an advertorial that did not add some sort of value to their readers' lives; the value exchange was paramount.

Advertorials continued to be a key feature of print advertising throughout most of the twentieth century. They were updated with the times, of course, becoming more visual as photographs became common in print, as well as more colourful as colour printing became prevalent, particularly in magazines.

There are countless examples of advertorials, sponsorships and various commercial content slots running across multiple publications throughout the twentieth century. There were some good, some bad and a whole bunch of mediocre examples in existence. Like today, there were myriad different formats and styles, depending on publication.

Did you know, for example, that the *New Yorker*, which is famous for its stylish cartoons, used to run similar cartoons as advertising in the 1950s? They were labelled 'Advertisement' at the top, but that was all. There was no additional disclosure or ad choices logo to inform readers. Surely there's very little difference, then, between what the *New Yorker* was doing nearly 60 years ago and what most modern publishers – *The Independent*, *Newsweek* or the *New York Times* – do today with native advertising. You'd think not. But for many that like to hark back to the pre-digital age of publishing with rose-tinted spectacles, there is, apparently, a difference.

The Guinness Guide to Oysters

One of the earliest examples of native advertising that you see referenced is David Ogilvy's famous *Guinness Guide to Oysters* (1950). He wrote about it in his popular *Confessions of an Advertising Man*,[4] explaining how he got the idea while travelling by train from New York City to his home in Connecticut. The idea is simple – and very common to content marketers and native advertisers today – but in 1950 it was a revolution. Instead of promoting how amazing Guinness was as a product, Ogilvy and his copywriter Peter Geer created content that gave valuable insight into nine varieties of oyster. The oysters were illustrated, and descriptions and information on each appeared beneath. Of course there was reference to Guinness within some of the copy – and a bottle of Guinness adorns the bottom right of the guide; for example: 'Oysters go down best with Guinness, which has long been regarded as the perfect complement for all seafood.'

But there were also long passages of interesting copy:

> Greenport: These oysters have a salty flavor all their own. They were a smash hit with the whalers who shipped out of Greenport in olden days. Oysters contain iron, copper, iodine, calcium, magnesium, phosphorous, Vitamin A, thiamine, riboflavin and niacin. The Emperor Tiberius practically lived on oysters.[5]

You can almost imagine, can't you – in the days before Wikipedia – a New York commuter reading the above passage from the ad in a magazine, saving the page and sharing these snippets of information about oysters with his family over dinner when returning home. Simplistic perhaps: but I would almost certainly bet that many men – and it was largely only men commuting in the 1950s – did just that as a result of reading this ad.

The Guinness Guide to Oysters is, essentially, a piece of native advertising, before the phrase existed. Many describe it as content marketing before content marketing. You could argue it is this, too, but given that Ogilvy distributed this content via paid-for media, and it was ultimately created to be distributed as an advertisement – not as a piece of content for a catalogue or company guide, for example – make this native advertising before it is anything else.

Native advertising is nothing new

Native advertising as a concept is not new. In terms of creating the assets – the content, or story – advertisers have been doing this for a century or more. Delivery and execution have changed as new technologies, ideas and tastes have developed. This is, as set out in the introduction to this book, why native advertising is not to be viewed as a revolution – something completely new that has been thrust upon us by digital advertising people and Silicon Valley technologists – but rather an evolution of ad formats and commercial processes that were well in place long before the internet came into existence.

Where the phrase came from

Credit for coining the term native advertising is generally believed to belong to venture capitalist Fred Wilson. Wilson is the co-founder of Union Square Ventures, a venture capital firm based in New York that has invested in numerous digital businesses, including Twitter, Tumblr, Foursquare, Zynga and Kickstarter.

Wilson is credited with referencing the phrase at the OMMA Global conference in 2011, where he described a new form of advertising as 'native monetization systems' for web properties. In his talk, Wilson explained how advertising had become tailored to particular platforms, as they had better performance when they were made to function as part of a site. He high-lighted Google paid search results, Facebook 'likes' and promoted tweets on Twitter among good examples at the time of 'native monetization systems'. It's an interesting talk. If you are interested in hearing more, you can watch it at www.avc.com/2011/09/the-fragmentation-of-online-marketing-1

Native monetization systems develop

BuzzFeed is often seen as the poster-child for native advertising, largely because it makes all of its revenue from native ads. But BuzzFeed only signed their first content deal in 2010. Back then, BuzzFeed did not refer to what it did as native advertising. It's only since 2011 that native advertising has morphed into the large, catch-all phrase that covers what we have today.

Sponsored stories hit the feed

In December 2011 Facebook announced that from 2012 'sponsored stories' would start appearing within the newsfeed of users across the web version of its website. Josh Constine's TechCrunch analysis of what the launch of in-feed advertising would mean for advertising as whole was uncannily accurate:

> If Facebook can weather the protest of users who want an ad-free news feed, it will have managed to open a significant new revenue stream... Sponsored Stories news feed ads could help Facebook steal ad spend from paid search and traditional display such as Google AdWords and AdSense.[6]

Although Facebook itself did not call this rollout 'native', now that the phrase 'native' was in the popular lexicon of digital marketing, its use spread to describe the growing appearance of 'native' formats such as these.

2012: the native advertising buzz builds

Native was the convenient term industry commentators, researchers and trade associations were looking for in order to classify this new form of advertising. In 2012, BIA/Kelsey began to reference this format as native when they published a report that predicted the rise in spend of 'social native ads' by 2016.[7] Dan Greenberg, Sharethrough CEO, also helped popularize the phrase when he published an article on TechCrunch in May 2012 entitled 'Five ways native monetization is changing Silicon Valley'.[8]

Native advertising in the UK

To illustrate how quickly the native market has grown in the UK, I want to highlight an episode from 2013. In early 2013 I wrote one of the first 'native ad' pieces that appeared in the UK for *Marketing Week*: 'Native content growth means brands have big opportunities'.[9] For at least a year afterwards – to my ongoing surprise – whenever I searched the term 'native advertising' in the UK version of Google, my article appeared in the top four or five results. No one was using the term in the UK. No one was talking about it. This all changed rapidly, of course, from the end of 2013 onwards.

2013 and onwards

From 2013 native advertising has become a well-known industry term. Helped by the digital-tech industry's buzzword machine – where countless articles, blog posts and thought-leadership pieces started carrying the phrase (in the US trade press mainly) – native advertising as a term stuck. 'Native' gained further industry-wide respectability in 2013 with the launch of the IAB *Native Advertising Playbook* and the FTC hosting a 'native advertising workshop'.

Endnotes

1   Marr, A (2005) *My Trade: A short history of British journalism*, Pan, London

2   *Arizona Republican* (15 December 1911) Advertisement for Arizona Weather [online] http://chroniclingamerica.loc.gov/lccn/sn84020558/1911-12-15/ed-1/seq-8.pdf [accessed 27 March 2017]

3   Hansen, RJ (2014) *The Arizona Republic*, Arizona invites Chicagoans to 'warm up' with ad blitz [online] www.usatoday.com/story/news/nation/2014/01/08/arizona-ad-blitz-targets-chicago/4369197/ [accessed 27 March 2017]

4   Ogilvy, D (2011) *Confessions of an Advertising Man*, Southbank Publishing, London

5   *Guinness Guide to Oysters* (1950) Available at: http://speakagency.com/wp-content/uploads/2013/03/oysters.jpg [accessed 27 March 2017]

6   Constine, J (20 December 2011) Facebook sponsored story ads to appear in the web news feed in 2012 [online] https://techcrunch.com/2011/12/20/sponsored-stories-news-feed/ [accessed 27 March 2017]

7   Heine, C (26 November 2012) Social media ads go 'native,' will hit $9.2b by 2016 [online] www.adweek.com/digital/social-media-ads-go-native-will-hit-92b-2016-145413/ [accessed 27 March 2017]

8   Greenberg, D (12 May 2012) Five ways native monetization is changing Silicon Valley [online] https://techcrunch.com/2012/05/12/5-ways-native-monetization-is-changing-silicon-valley/ [accessed 27 March 2017]

9   Lovell, D (20 March 2013) Native content growth means brands have big opportunities, *Marketing Week* [online] www.marketingweek.com/2013/03/20/native-content-growth-means-brands-have-big-opportunities/ [accessed 27 March 2017]

The global native advertising market

05

Since 2012 native advertising has emerged as a major player in the digital advertising economies of most established advertising markets. It's growing at a phenomenal rate as more and more advertising budget is moved into the format. Depending on which studies you read, native advertising accounts for somewhere between 10 and 20 per cent of existing digital display advertising budgets already. But this is set to grow even further over the next few years.

Why? There are many factors driving this growth – most of which we discuss in more detail throughout this book. Native advertising works – and the technology to run more and more sophisticated native advertising campaigns, at scale, is now more or less at advertisers' fingertips. But even if we ignore these product benefits, which are significant, there are other factors that lie behind the phenomenal growth we have seen to date, and why native advertising is poised to grow, overtake and eventually subsume the vast majority of the digital advertising space.

Digital trends signal native ad growth

Native advertising is unique in that it sits at the crossroads of many digital trends, which points towards rapid adoption of the format. We've gone into more detail on this and the many reasons why native advertising is so important in other chapters of this book. But to simplify the reasoning – and to highlight the momentum that native advertising has behind it – we can look at two major trends. These are:

1 **The rapid adoption of mobile browsing:** We live in a mobile-first publishing world. Most content is now consumed first on a mobile device; desktops are well and truly in second place. Native advertising is the only

advertising format that works well on mobile. Is mobile browsing going to decline in the near future? I'd place a large bet against it; wouldn't you?

2 **Content marketing:** Brands recognize that they, too, can create and publish great content that will generate engagement with their target customers. Today brands can create content easily, and distribute it at scale. With or without native advertising, that genie is out of the bottle: the days when publishers were the only avenue to audience for a brand are over. And content marketing is here to stay. Native is the natural accompaniment to distributing this content.

'Native advertising looks like a rare win-win for the industry: more effective for advertisers, more valuable for publishers, and more acceptable for users,' says Joseph Evans, digital media analyst at Enders Analysis. 'Its suitability for mobile, social, and video contexts means that growth in native will contribute the large bulk of increased digital display spend.'[1]

The global native advertising market by 2020

Analysis of the global native advertising market, based on figures from BI Intelligence, the Internet Advertising Bureau (IAB) and eMarketer, estimates that global investments in native advertising will reach $85.5 billion in 2020.[2] To put this whopping number into perspective, this means that by 2020, native advertising will account for 30 per cent of all digital ad spend globally, and that from 2016–20, the native advertising market will grow 213 per cent. Similar research conducted by Yahoo! and Enders Analysis in 2016 suggested that native advertising would grow by 156 per cent by 2020, and that native advertising would be the dominant format of digital advertising across Europe, where it will take a 52 per cent share of total European digital display advertising by 2020.[3]

Native advertising growth will run hand in hand with mobile advertising growth. The *BI Intelligence Digital Media Ad Spend Report* predicts that mobile will be the fastest-growing ad channel by 2020, rising by an estimated 26.5 per cent CAGR (compound annual growth rate) by 2020.[4] In addition, the report states mobile display ads, such as banners, will surpass desktop display-related spending even earlier, in 2017. So mobile advertising is on the up. But what is perhaps most interesting is that BI

Intelligence estimates predict that it will be native advertisements that will account for 63 per cent of all total mobile display advertising by 2020, up from 52 per cent in 2015. This 9 per cent rise in market share will come over a five-year period when the overall mobile ad market as a whole is also growing by more than a quarter. So the growth in native advertising is significant.

The global market as a whole is going to grow, but there are differences between different markets. Let us take a look at them in more detail.

North America

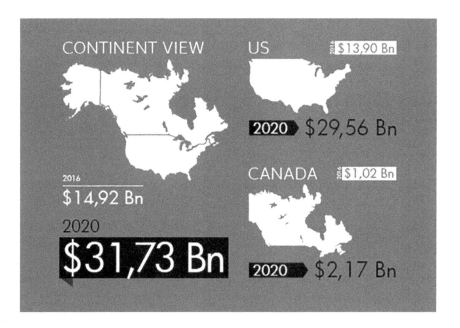

In 2020, North America will still be the biggest native advertising market in the world, with investments reaching $31.7 billion. The US market will dominate, where it will be worth $29.65 billion – up from $13.9 billion in 2016. The Canadian market will double in size by 2020, to be worth $2.17 billion, up from $1.02 billion in 2016. North America will account for 37 per cent of the global growth in native advertising.

Asia and the Pacific

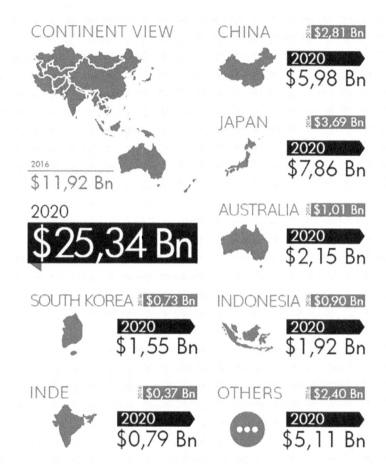

CONTINENT VIEW

2016
$11,92 Bn

2020
$25,34 Bn

CHINA   2016 $2,81 Bn
2020
$5,98 Bn

JAPAN   2016 $3,69 Bn
2020
$7,86 Bn

AUSTRALIA   2016 $1,01 Bn
2020
$2,15 Bn

SOUTH KOREA   2016 $0,73 Bn
2020
$1,55 Bn

INDONESIA   2016 $0,90 Bn
2020
$1,92 Bn

INDE   2016 $0,37 Bn
2020
$0,79 Bn

OTHERS   2016 $2,40 Bn
2020
$5,11 Bn

Asia and the Pacific is perhaps a few years behind the North American and European market when it comes to native advertising, but the potential is vast. Over the next few years we can expect major advances in the Asian native advertising space. The market as a whole is estimated to be worth $20.34 billion by 2020, up from $11.92 billion in 2016.

In most countries in the region, native advertising is predicted to more than double over a four-year period. The native advertising market in China will be worth $5.98 billion, up from $2.81 billion. Japan, the largest ad market in Asia, is set to see the native advertising market reach $7.86 billion by 2020, virtually doubling the $3.69 billion-a-year industry it is today. The market in South Korea will increase to $1.55 billion from $0.73 billion; the Indian market will grow from a modest $0.37 billion to $0.79 billion; and the market in Indonesia will increase from $0.90 billion to $1.92 billion. Meanwhile the Australian market will grow from around $1 billion today to be worth $2.15 billion by 2020. Asia and the Pacific will account for 30 per cent of native advertising growth to 2020. The opportunity for native advertising across this region is staggering.

CASE STUDY Social media native advertising: Teman Nabati and Twitter

Teman Nabati (@TemanNabati) is an Indonesian snack food company famous for their biscuits and crackers – notably for children. When Teman Nabati was looking to extend their reach to young Indonesian professionals in the 25–35-year-old age range and build brand awareness, they turned to Twitter native advertising.

Teman Nabati worked with Klix Digital (@KlixDigital) to create their Twitter ad campaign. The focus of the campaign was clear and distractions within their promoted tweets were kept to a minimum.[5]

Example tweets included:

Follow our account, Nabati, the snack to go with coffee, and follow our monthly quiz to win exciting gifts from us!

A/B testing of the tweet copy was instrumental in the campaign's success. New copy and interest group targeting was tested each week.

Results

- 42 per cent over follower growth goal;
- 10,000+ engaged followers that are interested in our products.

Why it worked

Simple messaging, and continual testing of creative and interest groups were instrumental in increasing the Twitter following of this brand. With continued focus on week-to-week optimization, Teman Nabati was able to identify what worked and improve the performance of the campaign, growing an engaged audience that has an interest in their products.

Europe

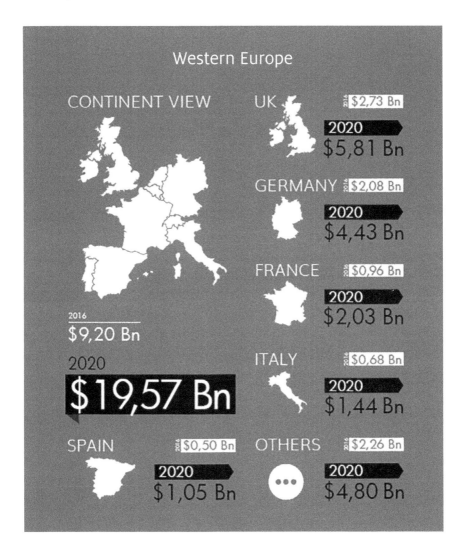

Across Europe, native advertising is growing apace. From a strong base in markets such as France, Germany and the UK, native advertising is on course to grow by $10 billion by 2020, to be worth nearly $20 billion per annum, up from $9.2 billion in 2016.

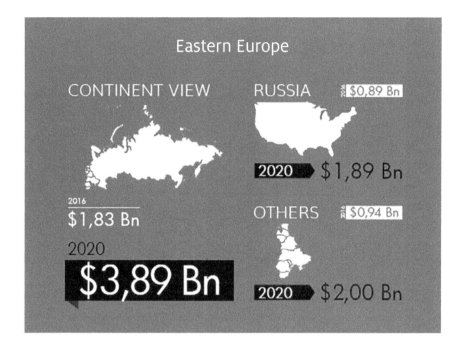

The UK is predicted to be the largest native advertising market – up to $5.81 billion by 2020, from $2.73 billion in 2016. The market in Germany will follow, where it is estimated to be worth $4.43 billion by 2020, up from $2.08 billion in 2016. The French market is set to more than double, up from $0.96 billion in 2016 to an estimated $2.03 billion by 2020. Italy and Spain – the remaining 'big five' ad markets in Europe – are tipped to be worth $1.44 billion and $1.05 billion annually by 2020. Russia, meanwhile, is also tipped to increase its native ad market from $0.89 billion in 2016 to $1.89 billion annually by 2020. Western Europe will account for 23 per cent of total native advertising growth to 2020.

CASE STUDY Social media native advertising:
Moeble.de and Facebook

Moebel.de[6] is Germany's leading furniture and home decor search portal. It serves millions of Germans each month, seeking out a host of relevant items from a large range of online retail partners.

Moebel.de was looking to boost quality traffic to retail partner sites, with the overall aim of increasing conversions. Their online marketing agency hurra.com adopted a phased approach using Facebook advertising products. The phased approach involved, first, using Facebook link ads and carousel ads within Facebook users' newsfeeds to reach a wide audience. Retargeting was then used via website custom audiences to retarget specific ads to those who had already visited the Moebel.de website or the brand's Facebook page.

But in addition to this, an advanced website custom audience focused on people who had visited Moebel.de several times in the previous 30 days, thereby showing a very high level of purchase intent.

Results

- reduced cost per conversion by almost 25 per cent by using advanced website custom audiences to drive high-quality traffic to its partner sites;
- 22% lower cost per acquisition;
- 16% boost to click-through rate;
- 17% lower cost per click.

Why it worked

This is a good example of how brands and their agencies can use native advertising content to increase audience share, but to also increase the sales funnel. It's a good example of campaign phasing; at one point 'spreading the net wide' to reach a large audience, and then using the data available to all digital marketers to retarget those users who have expressed some level of intent to buy. By tailoring ads to the behaviour of people, combined with great use of user data, hurra.com demonstrated significant business results – a 25 per cent reduction in cost per conversion is an outstanding campaign outcome.

Central and Latin America

CONTINENT VIEW

2016
$1,72 Bn

2020

$3,66 Bn

BRAZIL $0,93 Bn
2020
$1,97 Bn

ARGENTINA $0,25 Bn
2020
$0,53 Bn

MEXICO $0,18 Bn
2020
$0,39 Bn

Just like the Asian market, the Latin American market is perhaps a few years behind North America and Europe, but that doesn't mean that there is no opportunity there. In many ways Latin America is a major opportunity for native advertising. The fact that there are only two major languages – Spanish and Portuguese – and numerous publishing groups, agencies and service providers that operate in a pan-continental fashion, mean that native advertising uptake, when it does take root, will be swift. Perhaps this is why the Latin American digital advertising market is predicted to be worth $3.66 billion by 2020, up from $1.72 billion in 2016. The major markets of Brazil, Argentina and Mexico are likely to drive this growth. The Brazilian market is predicted to be worth $1.97 billion by 2020, up from $0.93 billion in 2016; Argentina $0.53 billion, up from $0.25 billion; and Mexico $0.39 billion, up from $0.18 billion.

Interview with Agustin Coll, CRO and Co-Founder, Headway

Headway is a leading company in developing marketing powered by technology. NativeWay, powered by Headway, is a revolutionary technology to run native ad formats that matches the look and feel of each publisher's site in Latin America. The two formats available are Native Content and Mobile Native Content. You can see more at www.nativeway.co.

Headway have operations all around the world and 18 offices located in: US (San Francisco, Miami), Mexico (Guadalajara, Mexico City), Guatemala (Guatemala City), Dominican Republic (Santo Domingo), Costa Rica (San Jose), Panama (Panama City), Colombia (Bogota), Ecuador (Quito), Peru (Lima), Paraguay (Asuncion), Brazil (Sao Paulo), Chile (Santiago), Uruguay (Montevideo), Argentina (Buenos Aires), Spain (Barcelona), and Israel (Tel Aviv).

How big is native advertising in your market?

Latin American programmatic is entering the second phase of evolution, past the basic understanding of networks and audiences. There has been a 'hole' in native advertising that has left clients searching for better ways to communicate with targeted audiences.

What do you like about native advertising?

What we really like about native advertising is that instead of banners, you are seeing a sponsored article or link to an interactive experience or video: something relevant in a relevant context.

Do publishers understand properly what native advertising is?

Yes, we're willing to educate them so that they understand the benefits of partnering with us and venturing into the universe of native advertising.

Do you think native advertising is likely to grow in your market?

We are more than confident in the effectiveness of native advertising, confirming that the ads consistently surpass CTR (click-through rate) standards while ensuring that ads are seen by people that care about them in a relevant context. When done right, native ads have proven to generate high click levels and traffic because the reader is drawn into the experience presented in the highly relevant ad.

What is the most common question you get asked about native advertising by clients?

People mostly ask if they need to choose between traditional or native formats. Brands and publishers are not forced to pick traditional or native: they can use NativeWay while maintaining traditional ads such as banners as well.

What, if any, do you think are the barriers to native advertising growing in your market?

Publishers are used to creating sites with spaces for banners that they monetize, but when you offer them the opportunity to show content automatically, the biggest challenge is to change the paradigm of leaving spaces open on the site for ads.

Headway works with trading desks and advertisers to help each client to find the most adaptable sites. This is innovative because the trend is to use traditional formats for programmatic: typically, programmatic does facilitate native ads; in this sense clients can target as specifically as they want. We need to help publishers to better understand that they do not have to modify their existing pages, but they do need to make the few technical changes necessary to run a native ad campaign and select where on the page they want the ad to appear.

Africa

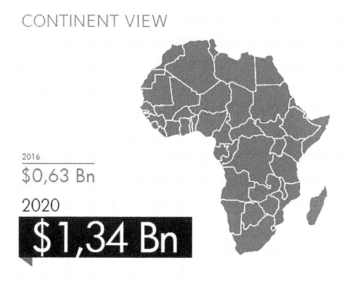

CONTINENT VIEW

2016
$0,63 Bn

2020
$1,34 Bn

The native advertising market across the African continent is growing, with markets such as South Africa, Kenya and Nigeria leading the way. It is very much in its infancy here, but the continent has much potential. Native advertising should in fact become the main digital ad format of Africa by 2020. Why? Africa is a mobile-first digital landscape. Mobile e-commerce and mobile ads are big business across the continent. Native advertising is the natural ad format for mobile devices. The number of mobile subscribers across Africa is predicted to grow to 720 million by 2020. The number of smartphones across Africa almost doubled from 2014 to 16, reaching 226 million consumers, according to a report published by GSMA on Africa's mobile economy.[7] In 2016, for example, *We Are Social* reported that 75 per cent of all webpages served in South Africa were to mobile devices.[8] As prices for smartphones continue to fall, more and more Africans will undoubtedly be using them – and as a result increasingly interacting with native advertising.

Notes

1 Leggatt, H (24 February 2016) Native ads to dominate display ad spend by 2020, *Biz Report* [online] www.bizreport.com/2016/02/native-ads-to-dominate-display-ad-spending-by-2020.html [accessed 27 March 2017]

2 ADYOULIKE (30 January 2017) Native to be 30 per cent of global ad spend by 2020 [online] www.prnewswire.com/news-releases/adyoulike-research-native-to-be-30-of-global-ad-spend-by-2020-612122003.html [accessed 27 March 2017]

3 Degun, G (23 February 2016) Native ads in Europe to grow by 156 per cent [online] www.campaignlive.co.uk/article/native-ads-europe-grow-156-per-cent/1384650 [accessed 27 March 2017]

4 Meola, A (no date) Here's why native ads will take over mobile by 2020, *Business Insider* [online] www.businessinsider.com/heres-why-native-ads-will-take-over-mobile-by-2020-2016-4?IR=T [accessed 27 March 2017]

5 Twitter (no date) Teman Nabati success story [online] https://business.twitter.com/en/success-stories/teman-nabati.html [accessed 27 March 2017]

6 Facebook (no date) Success Stories: Moeble.de [online] www.facebook.com/business/success/moebel-de [accessed 27 March 2017]

7 Springham, J (26 July 2016) Africa hits 557M unique mobile subs; smartphones to dominate by 2020 [online] www.mobileworldlive.com/featured-content/home-banner/africa-hits-557m-unique-mobile-subs-smartphones-to-dominate-by-2020/ [accessed 27 March 2017]

8 Shezi, L (no date) SA's 26 million internet users spend almost three hours a day on social media [online] www.htxt.co.za/2016/04/29/the-stuff-south-africa-26-8-mil-internet-users-spend-most-their-time-doing-online/ [accessed 27 March 2017]

PART TWO
How can native advertising impact your business?

The different types of native advertising

06

Native advertising can mean different things to different people. It's something of an umbrella term. Native advertising touches upon many different aspects of the existing media landscape. It's disrupting, blurring and amalgamating many product sets: creating hybrid models that are difficult to categorize, constantly in flux and a challenge to pin down – a bit like the digital industry as a whole, don't you think? Which is yet another reason why native advertising is the go-to advertising medium for digital.

It's the impetuous, plucky start-up ad medium that tears up the rulebook, seeks out disruption and challenges existing ways of doing business. Its fluidity means it can adapt to the changing needs of digital. It also means that there is almost a Velcro-like ability for different terms, categories and sub-categories that exist in the wider digital world to be applied to native advertising, too. This can and does cause considerable confusion.

Branded differentiators and digital marketing

Every year there are new phrases in digital. They can appear almost overnight: a new phrase is coined – normally by one or two specific entrepreneurial businesses and their marketing teams – that seems to answer a specific dilemma marketers face, or describes a specific type of activity, which may have been going on for a long time already. But now it has been given a new classification that the industry understands. Or they think they now understand.

Once a phrase or term is coined to describe some specific digital activity, you can bet your house on it that the process will start all over again around that specific term, splintering off into myriad different sub-categories of that specific term to create new branches and sub-sets.

This happens continually in digital, less so in many other industries. One of the other industries I can think of with so many different modes of categorization is modern dance music. If you are new to the business of digital, it may be a good analogy to use before getting into the specifics of native advertising.

If we look at dance music, we can break its categorization down into something like the following:

- Popular music – no one can deny that dance music is not part of 'popular' music. Dance music is music.
- Dance music – this categorizes the music created in a specific genre, or category of popular music. All music created electronically with a particular fast beat, as a very loose definition, falls into this category.

It makes sense to break dance music down into a separate category (or genre) away from all other types of popular music, doesn't it? Otherwise, when you're looking to buy, you'd have your One Direction pop songs mixed up with your John Digweed and David Guetta dance anthems.

So far, so simple. But this is where it gets interesting. Under the umbrella of 'dance music' – the broad category – we have (and this is not exhaustive) more sub-categories:

- house;
- techno;
- trance;
- dub step;
- drum n bass;
- garage.

These are distinct sub-categories of dance music, which over time have grown so large to almost become categories of music of their own: but their root is still dance music.

But it doesn't end there. If we take 'house' as an example, within this sub-category alone we have more 'sub-sub-categories' – and again, this is non-exhaustive. We have:

- acid house;
- tech house;
- electro house;
- tribal house;

- progressive house;
- deep house;
- hard house;
- trance house.

So to get to 'tech house', the journey in terms of categories looks like this:

Popular Music → Dance Music → House Music → Tech House

In order to understand and recognize when you hear a 'tech house' song being played to you, as a consumer you need to be:

- at first, familiar with what dance music sounds like;
- know the difference between what house music sounds like, in comparison with, say, drum n bass;
- and third, you need to know how to be able to recognize the difference between what tech house sounds like and progressive house to deep house, for example.

If you follow these steps, you can quickly see that when you get down to the sub-category and sub-sub-category levels of dance music, it's only the most avid dance music aficionado that is capable of making a clear differentiation between, say, tech house and deep house.

This level of differentiation, which is often minimal to the unfamiliar, happens again and again in digital.

Why?

One of the main reasons for this categorization in digital stems from expertise and familiarity. In an ever evolving space, digital marketing is always changing – businesses and products are always adapting what their products and services are. To remember everything, you need an almost encyclopaedic knowledge base to differentiate one product from the next, and one business from another. To help the industry manage this, it often needs to rely on labels.

But there are also enormous benefits to categorization for businesses in digital. The gatekeepers of advertising spend are traditionally planner–buyers. Media agencies (and more recently programmatic trading desks) sit on millions and millions of dollars of advertiser spend – and for any new or existing media business, success or failure depends on getting 'on plan'.

But how do you differentiate yourself from your would-be competitors, pivot your existing business to maximize an opportunity around a specific new product, or dislodge an incumbent that has huge market share?

Planner–buyers have to chop up and allocate ad spend somehow, and these categories offer convenient ways for them to feel comfortable in ring-fencing budgets. So if you create a new, must-have ad sector for your business, it's logical to presume your business will get on a plan.

Businesses, particularly new advertising and marketing technology businesses, are keen to 'own' a category all for themselves for this reason. Why? It's far more profitable to say that you are a leader in a specific category, no matter how niche (remember, in the digital ad ecosystem, even the small niches can scale globally to be worth billions in ad revenue), rather than admit that you are the tenth-best or, heaven forbid, the twentieth-best company operating in a larger category. Likewise, businesses that may see an opportunity to pivot their existing operations towards a growing sector, category or sub-category may also generally always look to 'own' a new category with a strategic rebrand. In an industry full of marketers, this often happens.

It's what brand experts refer to as 'branded differentiators'. Brand expert David Aaker says:

> A branded differentiator is a branded and actively managed branded feature, ingredient, technology, service, or program that creates a meaningful, impactful point of differentiation for a branded offering over an extended time period. It provides a way to own an innovation, provide credibility to it, and make communication easier and more memorable. When it is warranted, and that can be a question mark, it can be a powerful part of the brand portfolio.[1]

So creating your own category, sub-category, genre, or product differentiator is straight out of the 'how to build your brand' playbook. In a competitive digital landscape where the rewards are colossal, everyone is trying to build a brand differentiator.

If you can show scale, momentum and even a subtle product differentiation alongside 'owning' your category, as a start-up operation it's far easier to attract investment, talent and new business opportunity. You might just be the next big thing, after all.

If you look at any digital sector, you'll see this coming through time and time again. It's an indicator of a maturing market sector when you see these categories and sub-categories bubble up within your own category of digital.

Native advertising categories and sub-categories

This is what is happening within the native advertising sector today. We have popular terms such as branded content, content partnerships, in-feed distribution, native display, in-stream native, in-ad native, true native, premium native, content recommendation, content discovery, content widgets and many more phrases surfacing. Some have different, subtle differences; others mean the same thing.

These phrases can be confusing for anyone new that wants to gain a clear overview of the native advertising space. If you are confused, the first thing to remember is that you are not alone. For a while now, native advertising has been a catch-all term. In a space moving so fast – which loves to categorize and promote branded differentiators – this scenario was always going to happen.

Native advertising is at the stage now where all the hype has been replaced by recognition – and a once nice-to-have digital product on a media plan is now increasingly a must-have. A lack of clarity on the product set is a threat to the future success of native advertising, particularly as native advertising grows. If people don't understand it properly, how can they sell it in to their clients, buy it with confidence, maintain standards and nurture its growth?

Part of the reason behind this book is to try and cut through a lot of the 'noise' that surrounds native advertising at present; a simple Google search around native advertising can leave the uninitiated with more questions than answers. I sit on the Content and Native Council at the IAB UK, and have been part of ongoing discussions with brands, agencies and publishers around the categorization of native advertising formats for some time now. It's an ongoing discussion – but an important one for the native advertising market as a whole.

Native advertising product definitions

Below we will look at the existing native advertising product set – and how to potentially simplify it – so you really see how these different types of native can help your business. Defining the mechanics that go into different native advertising formats is a challenge. It's hard to pigeonhole something so fluid: something that can include anything from a promoted tweet on Twitter to an in-depth, interactive article on the *New York Times*; a search result on Google, to a product listing on Amazon; a promoted video on Facebook to an in-feed post promoting a how-to blog post. The fluidity of the product makes definitions difficult. But that hasn't meant that no one has tried to define it and break down its product offerings.

The Internet Advertising Bureau (IAB) playbook

The first attempt to offer a definition for native advertising was undertaken by the Internet Advertising Bureau (IAB). In December 2013 the US IAB released their *Native Advertising Playbook* with the aim of providing guidance to publishers, agencies and marketers on successfully leveraging native advertising in their campaigns.

The playbook laid a lot of the groundwork for how people in the industry view native advertising. Peter Minnium, Head of Brand Initiatives, IAB, explained at the launch the reasoning behind creating the playbook: 'The more we can define and structure the framework surrounding native advertising, the easier we will make it for brands to easily incorporate it into their ad buys.'[2] Or, as I'd maybe simplify it: 'If advertisers understand it better, they will buy more.' (I recommend everyone seek out and download the playbook at www.iab.com/wp-content/uploads/2015/06/IAB-Native-Advertising-Playbook2.pdf.)

The IAB playbook highlights six core interactive ad formats that constitute native advertising. These are:

1 in-feed units;

2 paid search units;

3 recommendation widgets;

4 promoted listings;

5 IAB standard ads with 'native' element units;

6 custom.

The IAB *Native Advertising Playbook* does a great job at setting out a universal definition for native advertising, but as the native advertising field has evolved, this model does have the potential for misinterpretation. This is in part because of advances in the lexicon since 2013 and the categories created.

While theoretically falling under native advertising, today's native advertising space is demanding a revamp. Let's look at each category in isolation:

The six IAB categories of native advertising

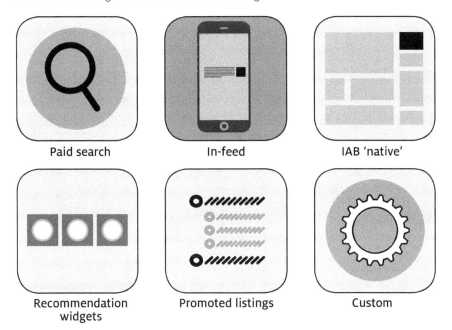

Paid search	In-feed	IAB 'native'
Recommendation widgets	Promoted listings	Custom

In-feed units

The playbook sets out that this category includes all in-feed units across social media platforms such as Facebook and other social media sites, as well as in-feed units across publisher websites.

- **Paid search units:** these units are concerned with Google Adwords search results and similar products from search engine pay-per-click results.

- **Recommendation widgets:** these are the now ubiquitous content recommendation units you see across publisher websites – often, but not exclusively, at the foot of article pages.

- **Promoted listings:** primarily these are product listings promoting specific products on marketplaces such as Amazon.

- **IAB standard ads with 'native elements':** you'd be right in failing to grasp immediately what this category refers to. It basically means banner ad formats – MPUs (multi-purpose units – the square boxes you see display ads appear in) and banners that run 'native elements'. What is meant by 'native elements'? Essentially, it's an ad that will appear in the defined IAB ad sizes (such as 300x250 pixels for an MPU), but will invariably be made up of a title, image thumbnail and description.

- **Custom:** again, this category is difficult to explain. It's the equivalent of saying 'other' – and that's what it is, really: a catch-all for all of those native elements, such as some bespoke native ad formats and units created by individual publishers and platforms, to run.

It's easy to see how these categories and classifications developed. The core definition of native advertising as 'advertising that matches the design of the experience they live in, looks and feels like natural content and behaves consistently with the native user experience', means that almost any sort of digital format, with a little bit of imagination, could fall under this umbrella term. But as a bid to see the wood for the trees on all things native, it can be misleading.

Paid search

If we take paid search listings, for example, few people would disagree that search listings such as Google Adwords results are forms of native advertising, but for the best part of a decade this entire sector was known as 'search' and 'paid search'. Ask any marketer what paid search is and they'll tell you 'paid Google ads'. Lumping search into native advertising in this way has confused the situation.

IAB standard units with native elements

Now let's look at IAB standard units with native elements, or rather, banner ads that look native. This has caused confusion in the market, too, largely because it is such a clunky term that very few people on first reading immediately understand.

When native advertising was first gaining in popularity, very few publishers had bespoke native ad placements set up: advertising was relegated to the fringes of their sites – in the banner slots. Today, the majority of premium publishers have native advertising units already set up across their publications: I know, because I helped a large swathe of these publishers create and position them. The internal debate about where native advertising should sit, what it should look like and the type of ads that come through on them has happened already. This wasn't the case in 2013.

The custom category, that catch-all term for 'other' native ad formats, leaves room for all sorts of misreading, too. If you are a chief marketing officer for a brand new to native advertising, you want to clearly understand the space. Does 'custom' really clarify it for you? I suspect not.

To some extent the 'custom' term was unavoidable – how else do you bucket very different product types together? But as times are changing, this is a good time to hone in on exactly what's out there and how improved definitions can help us.

It's worth reiterating the challenges faced in 2013. The playbook was a great introduction. But further definition has been needed to clearly define – and help grow – the native advertising space.

The Content and Native Definitions Framework

In May 2016, the IAB UK published the Content and Native Definitions Framework. The definitions framework split content and native advertising into main categories: brand-owned; publisher-hosted and/or made; and native distribution units. We'll summarize these below. The Framework is on page 65.

CASE STUDY Brand content: Pepsi MAX and BuzzFeed

In the summer of 2015 Pepsi MAX partnered with BuzzFeed Australia to increase awareness and grow audience in the Australian market. Together, Pepsi MAX and BuzzFeed AU created a series of articles. The content revolved around the 'summer' and the wider theme of fun. BuzzFeed created content designed to resonate with their Australian audience. Titles created included:

- 12 Things That Are Not Allowed This Summer
- 11 Epic Australian Places You Should Probably Visit Someday
- 13 Reasons Summer Is Your Best Friend
- 13 Hacks You Must Have In Your Life This Summer

The list-style content also included introductions such as 'Australia doesn't do nature by halves. Make sure you're living life to the MAX...'

Distribution involved the targeting of niche Australian groups on Facebook, studying user behaviour to keyword match and serve Facebook social media ad units to those more likely to engage with the Pepsi MAX BuzzFeed content.

Results

- 245,302 total views;
- 169,715 paid views;

- 75,587 social views;
- 1.4 times social lift;
- a total of 293 days consuming Pepsi MAX content;
- 16% average time on page for content compared with Australian average over same time period!

Why it worked

The content was created to appeal to a particular audience, at a particular time of year – the Australian summer. The content achieved these aims conclusively, but it also managed to align the brand – through well-made content – with the feelings and positive sentiment around the coming summer and 'fun'. The content created was not overly promotional – like the concept it wanted to promote, it too was 'fun'. Funny images and amusing 'life hacks' encouraged social shares and ongoing content consumption. Combining all of this with targeted audience extension via Facebook social media posts ensured that Pepsi MAX was able to grow and reach its intended audience and achieve its overall campaign objectives.

The difficulty of definitions

Navigating the different interests and how they all tie into the native advertising eco-system is challenging. Without the IAB lead in the US and UK, the native ad space would look even more disjointed, ill-defined and loose. It's an ongoing process that trade bodies, vested interests and the media industry as a whole can struggle to keep up with in the face of market forces, new technology and continued innovation in the digital advertising sector. We need to be aware that from the outside, looking in, marketers need to know what they are going to buy.

Simplifying the native advertising landscape

Over the next few pages I'm going to try to break down the native advertising market even further. This is my attempt to super-simplify what I see as the native advertising landscape that exists today.

IAB UK Content and Native Definitions Framework

| | Advertiser-owned | Media owner revenues (brand-based) | |
| | Brand-owned content | Hosted or made by publisher | Native distribution ad units |
	Owned	*Paid*	*Paid*
What it is, how it works, typical characteristics	Advertiser-owned and operated: conceived, made and managed eg website/app content elements (article, slides, video, app, social pages/sharing) contract publishing	**1 Publisher-controlled content*** (sometimes called 'supporter' or 'sponsored') • publisher-made, looks like surrounding editorial, enabled by brand but may have been produced even without brand funding • Publisher editorial control and sign-off **2 Advertiser-controlled commercial content** (sometimes called 'ad feature' or 'advertorial') • can be made by publisher and/or brand • advertiser editorial control and sign-off **3 Joint publisher/advertiser-controlled commercial content** (sometimes called 'ad feature' or 'advertorial') • can be made by publisher and/or brand, enabled by brand but may have been produced even without brand funding • publisher and brand editorial control • client consultation/publisher sign-off	Automated and programmatic (scale) content delivery. Examples include: • 3rd party aggregated • 3rd party curated • 3rd party discovery tools • 3rd party recommendation tools • in-ad (IAB standard ad formats)** • in-app • in-feed*** • proprietary/bespoke ad formats • promoted posts

(continued)

(Continuing)

| | Advertiser-owned | Media owner revenues (brand-based) | |
	Brand-owned content *Owned*	Hosted or made by publisher *Paid*	Native distribution ad units *Paid*
Brand purpose	Destination/Brand	Publisher content experience/partnership	Traffic driving / brand / publisher content experience / association
Pay basis	Content marketing / PR Budgets	Publisher rate card	Tenancy, CPE, CPC, CPA, CPM, CPL
Regulations	ASA CAP Code (Marketing Comms)	**1** may be subject to non-advertising regulatory/ industry codes eg IPSO **2** and **3**: ASA CAP Code	ASA CAP Code (Advertising)

Published courtesy of the IAB UK. iabuk.net/resources/standards-and-guidelines/content-and-native-definitions-framework-may-2016

NOTE Organic PR is excluded from these characteristics. Currently, paid search results and promoted listings are excluded.

* 'Publisher' includes influencers, for example bloggers and vloggers as well as traditional/digital media owners.

** IAB (US) Native Advertising Playbook, December 2013

*** In-feed Deep Dive (IAB US, July 2015)

The six categories of native advertising

1 search;

2 social;

3 product listings;

4 publisher partnerships;

5 in-feed native;

6 content recommendation.

The first three in my list are native advertising, yes, but – a bit like the house music in relation to dance music example – are pretty much their own categories already. Search, as outlined above, is well known, well documented and a colossal category of media in its own right. If you are reading this book to know more about search, you are reading the wrong book. There are hundreds, if not thousands, of books on search that you should turn to instead. So referencing search as native advertising, though theoretically correct, does nothing for clarity.

Likewise product listings. When I talk to anyone about native advertising, this format never comes up. If you work as a small business and access the Amazon marketplace, you may well use this format – but I suspect you never know it to be native advertising. So I think we can leave this category where it is for now.

In the categorization below I've also deliberately separated social media into a standalone category. Why? Again, it's a monstrous media category that operates on its own very comfortably already. Yes, social media ads are 100 per cent native advertising formats: but for marketers looking to hone and harness their native ad skills, and understand the landscape in which they will be operating, they need to differentiate, for example, between Facebook in-feed advertising and publisher programmatic in-feed native advertising. Calling a paid post on Facebook native advertising just confuses people; often it just causes barriers.

The main categories of native advertising you need to understand

This leaves just three main native advertising categories: brand content publisher partnerships; in-feed native distribution; and content recommendation. I would argue that the vast majority of people, when they think of native advertising, think of either one of these three categories, or social media advertising. They may not know the correct descriptions, but this is what they are thinking of. I'd guess this is what you are thinking, too.

The majority of news stories, blog posts and thought leadership you see with the term native advertising included surrounds these main categories or definitions of native. The chances are this is why you are reading this book. So it's these main categories we are going to focus on within this chapter, and largely throughout this book.

The native advertising pyramid

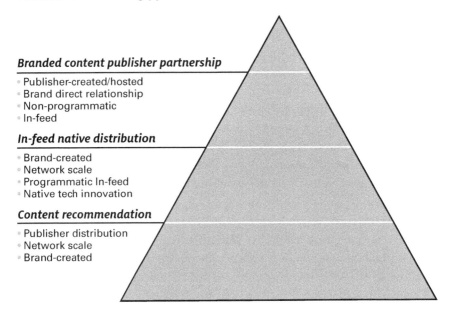

Branded content publisher partnership
- Publisher-created/hosted
- Brand direct relationship
- Non-programmatic
- In-feed

In-feed native distribution
- Brand-created
- Network scale
- Programmatic In-feed
- Native tech innovation

Content recommendation
- Publisher distribution
- Network scale
- Brand-created

1 Branded content publisher partnerships

This is a burgeoning native advertising sector. It goes under myriad different names – the IAB UK defines it, for example, as publisher-hosted and/or made. Others, including many publishers themselves, will call it branded content, or partner content, or publisher partnered content, or branded partner publisher content: the list goes on and on. For simplicity I've referred to it here as branded content publisher partnership. Why? Mainly because this type of native advertising – the type championed by the likes of BuzzFeed, the *New York Times*, Mashable, Quartz, *The Atlantic*, the *Telegraph*, the *Independent* and Germany's Burda Forward, to name just a few – is always publisher led.

At its core this form of native advertising involves a publisher creating a bespoke piece of content for a brand that is in keeping with the publisher's audience expectations and tone of voice. This native advertising format is, essentially, a partnership between one specific publisher and one specific advertiser. The content that is created is created more often than not by the publisher – increasingly by highly sophisticated internal commercial content teams, or studios – to ensure it meets specific audience expectations. This native content is then published and distributed across this specific publication. The advertising brand has sign-off on the proposal and the concept, but it's the publisher that leads the creative build and delivery.

Brand and publisher partnership

Typically, this type of native advertising is bought either by a brand directly with the publisher, for example by going directly to the *New York Times*; or by a brand's digital agency contacting the publisher on the brand's behalf. The key thing to remember is that they are point-to-point relationships. The booking is by agreed spend, and is based on insertion order, normally with a hefty lump set aside for creating the actual native content itself, in addition to the publishing of that content on a publication's website and/or other digital assets.

When a piece of publisher partnership native advertising is published, the preview to the ad will typically sit across a native advertising unit on the publication's website – say, a homepage, category page or article page. The preview normally looks like the preview of any other form of content on the site – it will have a title, a description and a thumbnail, for example. But it will also carry some labelling, so that readers know that the content is actually advertising. Most publisher partnership-created content is labelled with disclosure along the lines of 'sponsored by' or 'promoted by', or variations of this.

When the reader clicks on the preview, they are taken through to an editorial page on the same website, where the accompanying branded publisher partnership native advertising content sits. Again, the content on this page should always be properly labelled as sponsored or similar. But the crucial thing to remember is that the interaction with the advertising takes place within the publisher's environment, not the advertisers'. You interact with this native content on the publisher's website, surrounded by their other editorial messages and brand. You are still in the native environment you started off in. Publishers argue that allowing carefully crafted content messages into their space gives advertisers a strong opportunity to engage with publisher audiences in authentic ways, building trust and benefiting from prestigious editorial affiliation as a result.

Adherents argue that this publisher partnership style of native advertising is the only real form of native advertising that should exist because you are ensuring that the ad itself looks and feels like the surrounding editorial of the website in which it sits. But crucially, the native ad also speaks in the same language, tone and content style of the other content around it because it is also created by experts from those publications, who are adept in creating content in the right tone of voice for the audiences of these publications.

That's why when you read a piece of brand content on BuzzFeed, it's written and published in their 'listicle' house style, just like the majority of the rest of their content, rather than as a 1,000-word advertorial.

Publisher partnership and programmatic

It's worth noting that, as it stands, this bespoke branded content publisher partnership form of native advertising is currently not often bought, sold or traded programmatically. Standardizing the media-buying process for this type of native advertising is difficult, as when you embark on this sort of activity with publishers, as an advertiser, you are also paying for creative services and content creation. Quantifying time, creative energy and idea-generation down to standardized programmatically tradable marketing metrics is difficult (see Chapter 13, The Rise of the Content Studio). The creative cost is where most publishers make significant margin with their native advertising to date; so there is less incentive for many large-scale publishers to pursue a programmatic avenue for this format as it stands. However, native platform Nativo has recently enabled the programmatic buying of their 'true native' format programmatically, which could herald a change in this buy model in the near future.

To avoid any confusion, the previews for publisher partnership native advertising often can sit in-feed across a publication. In many instances publisher partnership previews and in-feed native advertising units (discussed below, as a separate native advertising category) do in fact occupy the same inventory space, but publishers normally prioritize their own publisher partnership native advertising ahead of third-party in-feed native advertising.

Publisher partnership native advertising summary

Also known as: brand content, ad partnership, true native, premium native:

- publisher created native content;
- typically hosted on one publication;
- direct one-to-one relationship between brand and publisher, or agency (on behalf of brand) and publisher;
- non-programmatic;
- previews can appear in-feed.

Major providers:

- all major publishers worldwide;
- technology providers include: ADYOULIKE, Polar, Nativo.

The truth about native labels

One of the latest additions to the native advertising lexicon is the phrase 'true native'. It may grow in use in the future. But what does it actually mean? True native is the phrase used to describe branded content publisher partnership native advertising – and the technology behind it.

The problem many have with the true native label is that it assumes, by definition, that all other types of native advertising are not true – which really is not the case. They are different, yes, but all native advertising products have their place in the marketer's toolkit.

Premium native

Another phrase that is growing in use is 'premium native'. This also refers to the brand content publisher partnership form of native advertising described above. So it means exactly the same thing as 'true native'. It is a less divisive phrase: the cost of running a bespoke publisher partnership native advertising campaign with a top publisher is, after all, considerably higher in most instances than what you would pay for in-feed native distribution or content recommendation, for example. Publishers, too, consider brand content and publisher partnership native advertising as their premium native advertising product.

CASE STUDY Brand content: UBS and the *New York Times*

UBS wanted to stand apart from the competition. So they launched Nobel Perspectives. The project's aim was to capture the great minds of Nobel laureates in the field of economic science, along with the ideas they've honed and championed throughout a lifetime of work.

As stated on the UBS Nobel Perspectives website (www.ubs.com/microsites/nobel-perspectives), 'We've committed to building an exclusive online library of interviews and analysis covering dozens of Nobel Laureates, their theories, their lives and the experiences that made them who they are.'

With background in mind, the *New York Times'* T Brand Studio and Mediavest collaborated with UBS for the creation of a multimedia interactive project looking into the current state and future of artificial intelligence through the lens of economic science. The challenge was to engage UBS's high net worth individual (HNWI) audience, who are notoriously elusive and time-poor.

Entitled 'AI: What It Takes to Be Human', the project linked to the work of the Nobel Laureate Herbert A. Simon and UBS's Nobel Perspectives marketing initiative.

To bring awareness to the UBS themes, a full and dedicated environment to AI was created so the reader could both learn and experience the complexity of the subject. This included:

- original reported article;
- chatbot experience;
- original photography;
- three Q&As – key experts;
- short doc video;
- interactive timeline.

Results

The results were available in real time, on the T Brand Studio dashboard:

- 217,593 page views;
- 133 social referrals;
- 196,000 uniques;
- 1 m 24 s average dwell time;
- 68.4% average video watched.

The project reached its target within the first month and achieved a total of over 200,000 page views, exceeding the client's and publisher's expectations. The average session time was also above T Brand Studio's benchmarks:

- 4 in 5 stated that content was a good fit with UBS;
- 80% recall achieved by the paid post in Asia/EU/US;
- 2 in 3 want to read more UBS content;
- 25–35% increase in brand favourability.

Why it worked

Creating content for high net worth individuals with little time has many challenges. The standard has to be extremely high in order to engage with this audience. The idea has to be strong, the execution even more so. This example works perfectly. To generate 133 social referrals from a group that do not share content lightly, in addition to an average dwell time of over one minute, illustrates that the content was captivating for the audience, reinforced by the fact that two in three readers expressed an interest in wanting to read more UBS content as a result. Why did it work? More than anything, it worked because the idea was a good one, the content created was relevant and interesting, and the environment in which it was showcased was appealing to the target audience. This is an outstanding example of branded content. The creative, the editorial and the design all combine to showcase branded content at its very best.

Find out more at: http://paidpost.nytimes.com/ubs/what-it-takes-to-be-human.html

2 In-feed native distribution

This category of native advertising is perhaps the area that needs the greater clarification of all within the category groupings. It's the style of native advertising that is all too easy to dismiss, or lump into other categories – or not fully understand. In the interests of full disclosure, this is the category where my business, ADYOULIKE, sits. This is the category I therefore know best. In fact, alongside my colleagues and a handful of people working for competitors, it's a native category I've helped create: bit by bit, publisher by publisher, integrating new native advertising units across the publishing landscape of Europe, the US and the world over. From inauspicious beginnings, this category of native advertising is now set to run to billions in ad revenue annually. It's already a key part in the digital revenues of some of the biggest publishing groups in the world. It's for this reason that in-feed native distribution needs to sit in its own category, separate from social media native advertising and the other main native ad formats.

What is in-feed native distribution?

When I'm asked to explain to people who do not work in media what I do, I normally go in with my basic elevator pitch, which is something like this:

> My business runs Facebook-style adverts across a network of publisher websites. The adverts are typically promoting interesting content – editorial or video. The adverts are normally positioned directly in-feed and will run across all devices; mobile, desktop and tablet.

That's my basic summary. I typically always lead with the Facebook-style element because almost everyone on the planet is familiar with what a Facebook ad looks like. And, in essence, that's what this category of native advertising does: it replicates the advertising style and uses the same assets as social media advertising, but moves it to the direct 'open web' publisher environment. They are bespoke native advertising units that seamlessly fit into the publications on which they appear – and can usually run all types of content asset – editorial, video and more.

Publisher voice versus brand voice

When you partner with a publisher for bespoke branded content native advertising, as an advertiser, it is all about accessing a publication's unique tone of voice and tailoring a marketing message for your brand to fit into that voice. In-feed native distribution, in comparison, offers an outlet for brands to directly share their own unique voice with a wide audience. In-feed native advertising is the format brands are increasingly choosing to distribute their own brand-created content. It's the conduit used to speak to your audience in your own voice – the voice of your brand – not through the voice of a publisher.

Brands spend millions on creating branded content annually – and while most brands will value publisher partnerships with leading publishers, there are many more times when they are keen to share the great content and advertising messages they've spent millions of dollars creating in their own unique voice, too. This is what they do on Facebook and other social media channels; in-feed native advertising allows them to do this across leading publications outside of social media too. In effect, it's about maximizing the opportunities brands have to promote themselves and engage with their target audiences in the feed.

The content that is run in-feed differs from that which runs in publisher partnership. It is, the vast majority of the time, created by the brand themselves. This is the distribution channel for that brand content.

CASE STUDY Native advertising in-feed distribution: Marriott Weekends

Marriott Weekends undertook research into the holidaying habits of modern-day Britons and revealed the rise of the 'micro-break' – quick, easy and super-local getaways.

In August and September 2016, Marriott looked to promote and raise awareness and consideration in the UK for micro-breaks. They were also looking to enhance and drive awareness of their 'Discover Your Weekend Self' campaign – giving the customer a reason to visit their properties across the UK. The target audience were between the ages of 18 and 35: singles, couples and families with children, and users in the market for short breaks/holidays/vacations in the UK.

Marriott took a new and innovative approach by creating a quiz, challenging customers to discover their 'weekend selves'. ADYOULIKE promoted the quiz using their Native Traffic distribution product to deliver the ad to in-market holiday/vacationers. Upon click-through the user was delivered to the quiz, and upon completion of the quiz, they can be defined as one of five 'Weekend Selves':

- Foodie Finder;
- Path Explorer;
- Destination Finder;
- Trend Tracker;
- Sensation Seeker.

Marriott also used ADYOULIKE's highly engaging Native Traffic in-feed placements to deliver users to the Marriott Weekends page to discover locations that fit with their 'Weekend Self' type and to book a weekend break.

Marriott also used ADYOULIKE's in-house content studio to create five bespoke articles based on the above 'Weekend Selves', highlighting key attractions and cities to visit local to their 54 UK hotels. This content was then seeded out using ADYOULIKE's Native Story product, enabling them to deliver bespoke content at scale.

Results

ADYOULIKE's in-feed placements delivered high engagement rates for the quiz and content pieces:

Native Story

- impressions: 2,813,011;
- dwell times: 4 m 50 s (11 m 53 s high).

Native Traffic

- impressions: 6,892,056;
- CTR (click-through rate): 1.16%.

Native Traffic (quiz)

- impressions: 3,214,464;
- CTR: 1.40%;
- total hotel bookings: 242.

Why it worked

The 'Weekend Self' concept resonates well with audiences. The creation of highly engaging content around this concept, including an interactive, fun quiz, was key in creating an ongoing narrative and affinity with the user. The additional use of highly engaging ad formats situated in-feed rather than in the periphery of the publisher environment delivered significant reach and excellent click-through rate (CTR). Delivery of the advertising messages to relevant audiences in the right content and contextually relevant environments was also key to success. The fact the campaign – which had a brand-building KPI (key performance indicator) – delivered 242 hotel bookings is also testament to the fact that native advertising delivers significant return on investment.

Building scale: technology and innovation

In-feed native distribution is geared for scale. Advertisers are predominantly large media agencies or their trade-desk partners. This category is dominated by specific in-feed native technology services such as ADYOULIKE, Sharethrough and TripleLift, which have a built-up network of publisher partners. The relationship is typically: agency – technology, not brand – publisher. The ability to scale and distribute native content quickly is important.

It's also the main category of native advertising that is programmatically traded. This is significant because, as programmatic trading grows ever more prevalent, there is only one way ad spend through these in-feed native ad units is going to go. Research from BI Insider published in 2016 predicted that native ads in-feed will make up the bulk of native ad revenue from 2016–21. The report estimates it to be worth $36 billion in the US alone.

Another significant point to note is that the technology platforms in this in-feed category continue to be responsible for the technological innovations in native advertising today. It is these businesses that have developed the programmatic native advertising landscape, effectively laying the 'pipes' and undertaking a lot of the behind-the-scenes plumbing necessary to connect native advertising units to the wider programmatic advertising demand market. It's also these businesses that have helped transition many popular advertising formats from social media platforms – autoplay in-feed video, for example – and made them easily accessible for publishers to monetize and use for themselves.

It's these businesses that continue to test and launch new products – such as artificial intelligence – to continue to improve the native advertising product capability. Increasingly, too, as more publishers recognize the value of partnering with specific native technologies, it is these platforms that power many publisher partnership native advertising campaigns, as they are increasingly the go-to native 'ad servers' and native content management systems being used by leading publishers.

One of the other benefits that many brands like about in-feed native units is the environment in which the ad units themselves are located. More often than not an in-feed native ad unit on a publisher website is a standalone unit – it is not surrounded by any other native ad units. All around it, in the feed, is editorial content.

In-feed native advertising summary

Also known as: in-stream native advertising, native display, programmatic native:

- content is typically created by a brand themselves;
- scale – the ability to distribute one piece of content, across multiple platforms;
- network-level relationships – the ability to run native advertising from a single point of entry;
- programmatic trading;
- in-feed placements across device;
- ability to run multiple assets – video and more;
- pioneers in native technology and innovation.

Major in-feed native providers:

- ADYOULIKE;
- Nativo;
- Sharethrough;
- TripleLift.

3 Content recommendation

Content recommendation widgets are incredibly successful forms of native advertising. If you are not familiar with the phrase, you almost certainly will be familiar with the product. Visit any leading news website, read to the bottom of the article, and more often than not you'll see a box of three, or six, or sometimes more, 'promoted stories' or 'related content' style articles. The boxes will usually carry an image and an enticing headline. When you click on the ad, you'll be taken through to a third-party website – often the site of another publisher – where you'll be encouraged to read the article and click through to additional content on-site. Content recommendation offers huge scale for marketers. You can pay just a few cents per click for a website visit, and have your content shared across thousands of websites. You only pay for the visit. It is usually not traded programmatically – but this is changing – and is typically operated via self-serve dashboards that you can load content and budgets into easily and effectively.

Some of the stats around content recommendation are very impressive. Outbrain claims that content recommendation visitors to a page view 100 per cent more pages per session than those coming from search engines and 165 per cent more pages per session than those coming to the content from social media. In terms of bounce rate, content recommendation is 23 per cent less likely to bounce than search traffic and 32 per cent less likely to bounce than social traffic.[3]

The argument goes that as content recommendation is normally run at the foot of content articles, those reading and clicking through to more content are already in 'content consumption' mode. So they are likely to read and consume the content promoted to them more.

Savvy marketers and publishers use content recommendation units to promote content to a wide audience – and to drive website visitors to their websites. Over the last few years or so this native ad format has become a crucial part of most marketers' toolkits. Why? Because it has huge scale, is affordable and is easy to set up and monitor. If used properly, it can complement your wider digital marketing activity and be a valued part of your arsenal in distributing good-quality content, at scale.

Content recommendation summary

Also known as: content discovery, content rec, content widgets:

- inexpensive to run: pay-per-click model;
- self-serve option for testing content;
- network-level reach.

Major content recommendation providers:

- Outbrain;
- Taboola;
- Revcontent;
- Plista.

CASE STUDY Content recommendation: Amura and Taboola

Amura is one of India's leading digital marketing businesses, with a focus on performance marketing. It has operations in Pune, Mumbai, Bangalore and Delhi. Many of its clients include some of India's largest realtor businesses.

In June 2015, Amura organized the first-ever Indian Realty Flash Sale (IRFS 2015), a four-day online real estate event showcasing properties across 15 cities and 50 top Indian developers. This was India's first online flash sale specifically for the real estate category.

The flash sale had on board almost 35 national-level developers showcasing properties across cities such as Mumbai, Delhi NCR, Bangalore, Pune and Chennai.

Amura used content marketing to promote the event, using Taboola to power its content distribution with the aim of reaching Indian real estate buyers globally. A key objective for this campaign was finding the right target buying audience, quickly, across the digital space and directing them to register interest – via e-mail and mobile phone data capture – on the Indian Realty Flash Sale (IRFS) website.[4]

Results

- by the end of the campaign, over 500 new registrations for IRFS;
- an average 10% boost in qualified traffic to the IRFS microsite during the sale period;
- creative headline, description and image combination testing optimization increased average CTR by over 20% throughout the sale;
- large audience reach to spread brand awareness amongst prospective buyers.

Why it worked

This is a great example of how to use content marketing and content recommendation services to drive conversions, whatever your industry. The ability to target a global market of interested buyers, at scale, with tailored, relevant content – at the right time – was key to the success of this campaign. Continued optimization around best-performing creative led to a significant increase in click-through rate, which is key to the successful outcome of any native advertising campaign.

Over 500 new registrations is a real, quantifiable business outcome that demonstrates the powerful impact content, distributed at scale to the right audience, can achieve. Plus, while the performance and direct response aspect of the campaign are impressive, the additional reach of the campaign in boosting brand awareness and the promotion of the flash sale should not be overlooked either.

Harnessing native advertising to your marketing needs

Hopefully now that we've explained a little bit more about the different types of native advertising products that exist today, you'll feel more comfortable discussing, testing and finding out more about how they can work for your business.

For marketer and publisher alike, it's not an either/or decision about what you wish to run: branded content publisher partnership, in-feed native distribution, social media advertising or content recommendation. All work in conjunction with one another, or independently. What you do will depend on your budget, your business and what you want to achieve. My advice is to test them all, review the results and see what works. In summary, the four main types of native advertising to understand, as discussed above, are:

1 branded content publisher partnership;

2 in-feed native distribution;

3 content recommendation;

4 social media advertising.

Interview with Justin Choi, Founder and President, Nativo

Nativo is a pioneer of native advertising. Based in Los Angeles, California, the technology platform brings together 400 of the world's largest media companies and 700 top brand advertisers to transform the way branded content is created, distributed, and measured.

Having been there at its beginning, what are the biggest developments you've seen in native advertising in recent years?

Early on, even if someone had heard the term 'native advertising,' no one really knew exactly what it was. There was zero consensus and people were confused how to define it. This is still a challenge today, but advertisers and their agencies have worked to understand it better by asking how native scales, whether it's a niche strategy, and how do you best measure its performance? Today, the savviest advertisers are beginning to ask if native can be a viable alternative to traditional display and pre-roll formats.

What labelling does Nativo employ for its ad units (for example promoted by, sponsored by)? Has this changed at all over time?

The beauty of native is its seamless user experience, but its power is drained completely if consumers feel deceived. This is precisely why Nativo goes beyond US Federal Trade Commission (FTC) guidelines by mandating dual disclosure. We require that all native ads are clearly labelled as sponsored content and separated from editorial. Nativo also requires the advertiser directly attributed as the source of the content.

Do you think agencies and brands 'get' native content finally?

We're still in early days, but advertisers and their agencies are really starting to approach native in a more strategic way rather than treating it as a new format to 'test'. Also, everyone is beginning to understand there are multiple formats that fall under the 'native' umbrella. Nativo spends a lot of time educating media buyers on the differences between click-in true native content, click-out native display, and the most effective ways to leverage native video.

What are your average CTRs for native campaigns?

Nativo regularly sees from 0.5% to 1% click-through rates on desktop and slightly higher results on mobile, but this is a misnomer. We contend that CTR is a legacy of display advertising and was never an effective metric to gauge campaign performance. Native executions provide a whole slew of metrics to measure consumer engagement and campaign performance. User engagement metrics such as scroll behaviour and time spent on content informs advertisers if a click resulted in true attention and absorption of the message. We also use other methods to identify what perceptions the content influenced. We are particularly excited about our 'content-to-conversion' programmes that tie native content to real-world business outcomes. Look for research about this from Nativo in 2017.

Will 'true native' and programmatic ever be compatible?

Yes. We've recently announced three new programmatic buying channels through an integration with The Trade Desk. It's a first-of-its-kind programmatic offering that enables advertisers and their agencies to activate dedicated programmatic budgets across Nativo's entire private exchange, delivering uninterrupted ad experiences to more than 201 million monthly unique visitors. The integration includes private marketplace (PMP), programmatic direct, and open RTB (real-time bidding) workflows that leverage the power of both platforms. The Trade Desk integration is the first of several that Nativo is launching in 2017.

How important do you think native advertising is to the revenues of publishers? Is native advertising here to stay?

In a media eco-system dominated by two monoliths, it's vital that publishers of the open web are offered healthy alternatives to help them scale to compete. The advent of programmatic hasn't been particularly good for publishers, and legacy formats such as display are even less effective in a mobile world. Native, especially click-in, represents a chance to hit reset on digital advertising. True native represents a new advertising paradigm that is respectful of consumers, protective of open web publishers, and highly effective for advertisers. In the US market, display is projected to peak in 2018 and then start its decline. According to *Business Insider*, by 2021, 75% of all digital dollars will go towards native formats.

What metrics do you see consistently being used by advertisers to measure the success of native advertising? Do you think native needs its own metric?

It depends on the native format. In the case of native display – native ads that click out to other sites – advertisers measure success just as they measure banners: clicks and traffic. True native, on the other hand, Nativo recommends looking at a combination of click rate and engagement metrics such as scroll depth and time spent. But we are really excited by the opportunity to measure success in terms of real-world business outcomes… did the content eventually drive more online and offline sales or actions? These are the ultimate measures for advertisers. In the meantime, we recommend advertisers use engagement signals in addition to click rates to see if their clicks are resulting in meaningful consumer attention.

What are the benefits, if any, for big name brands in using native advertising over other types of advertising?

True native formats allow advertisers to speak to consumers in more authentic, meaningful ways. This is why it performs better than other types of digital advertising. When consumers can engage branded content and editorial content seamlessly, the inherent value exchange between consumer and advertiser is honoured. It empowers brands to complement the editorial experience rather than interrupt it. Everyone wins in this scenario.

Native placements are in the feed or news well, so they provide greater visibility compared with display ad placements that normally sit to the right or top of the content. True native is better at engaging and influencing the consumer. It also works very well in mobile environments. It's the soft sell versus the hard sell of display ad formats and it aligns with the way consumers expect to be engaged. The format allows for brands to tell a deeper story to create intent, change minds and capture hearts. Contrast this with display campaigns, which are better at capturing credit than creating intent.

What do you see as the major challenges native advertising faces in the next few years?

Unfortunately, in the short term, I see display companies continuing to look for ways to worm their way from the outside rails into the content feed. There are a lot of companies offering publishers unhealthy alternatives that will erode the trust of their audiences. If bad user experiences, interruptive executions and aggressive targeting get associated with content, the opportunity to create a better advertising eco-system will be lost.

For the digital media eco-system to remain healthy, we cannot afford to see the demise of open-web publishers. And since advertising supports media and a free press, consumer access to a wide variety of quality content and viewpoints may also be negatively impacted. The major challenge is to scale the category without losing the qualities that make native ads a better alternative. At Nativo, we believe that we win when everyone wins. That's why we are putting everything we have into an advertising paradigm that is respectful of consumers, protective of open web publishers, and highly effective for advertisers.

Endnotes

1 Aaker, D (2014) *Aaker on Branding: 20 principles that drive success*, Morgan James Publishing, New York

2 IAB (12 April 2013) IAB releases native advertising playbook to establish common industry lexicon, evaluation framework & disclosure principles [online] www.iab.com/news/iab-releases-native-advertising-playbook-to-establish-common-industry-lexicon-evaluation-framework-disclosure-principles/ [accessed 28 March 2017]

3 Alex Bennett (3 April 2014) Brainpower: The online engagement battle is on – Discovery vs. search vs. social traffic [online] www.outbrain.com/blog/the-online-engagement-battle-is-on-discovery-vs-search-vs-social-traffic [accessed 28 March 2017]

4 Matt King (31 August 2016) Taboola generates over 500 new registrations for Amura in first-ever Indian realty flash sale [online] http://blog.taboola.com/taboola-case-study-discovery-generates-over-500-new-registrations-for-amura-in-first-ever-indian-realty-flash-sale/ [accessed 28 March 2017]

Who can benefit 07 from native advertising?

Native advertising can work for almost any business, across nearly any performance criteria, customer journey or sales cycle. In this chapter we will look to demonstrate how, whatever your business or purpose, native advertising can be a useful tool in your digital marketing toolbox.

The Association of Online Publishers (AOP), the voice of premium publishers in the UK, published research in March 2015, finding that nearly two-thirds (59%) of consumers find native advertising interesting and informative.[1] Native advertising works.

Whether you are a marketing manager at a large brand, looking to upskill on all things native, a small business owner looking for more exposure, or even a start-up operating on a limited budget, this chapter will show you how to harness this exciting advertising medium for your needs – without it costing you lots of money in the process.

Why native advertising?

Whether a big or small business, there are some key reasons why native advertising works:

- **Better engagement:** native advertising generally outperforms other types of digital advertising, particularly on mobile. Standard click-through rates for native advertisements continually hover around 1 per cent, but are often 2–3 per cent on mobile devices, depending on the campaign. Compare this with the average banner ad click-through rate of 0.05 per cent[2] and you can see why native advertising is so popular.

- **Better formats:** native advertising formats – that sit in, look and feel like the surrounding content of the page – are generally far better received by consumers than other forms of digital advertising, such as banner ads, pop-ups, or pre-roll video. They are non-interruptive, which means that as a format they do not anger consumers; so brands that advertise with this format naturally do not generate as much animosity.

- **Multi-asset execution:** 'brands as publishers' has been a common phrase in marketing for many years. All big brands, no matter what their industry, recognize the need to create relevant content as part of their marketing messages. This can involve the creation of reams and reams of content: short news stories, blogs, long-form editorial, interviews, infographics, quizzes, memes, photo galleries, white papers, PDF guides, interactive charts, videos, YouTube playlists, 360 photos, Instagram pages, Pinterest profiles, LinkedIn articles, 360 video, live streams. These are all just some of the types of content that big name brands continually produce on a scale that few publishers, let alone smaller brand competitors, could hope to compete against. But all too often a lot of this content is created – and used once – for one specific purpose (such as to promote an event on Facebook, or a sale, for example) and then not used again. Brands are literally sitting on treasure troves of great content that could be used for native advertising purposes. This is yet another great benefit of native advertising: you are not restricted by the type of content you run. All of the above mentioned examples could be repurposed and packaged to run as native advertising campaigns across platforms such as Facebook or Twitter, as well as in-feed across publisher platforms and content recommendation units. It's just as easy to run an ad promoting a great video story as it is to promote a native ad promoting a detailed industry white paper. What you run is not dictated by the format, as it is with other forms of digital advertising.

Convey complex information easily

For many brands, explaining in detail what their product does and how it can help you can be complex. Take financial services, for example. If you want to extol the virtues of your pension product to a specific audience, it's incredibly hard to do that just in a banner. But with native advertising you can. You might want to promote some long-form video content that explains the product, warts and all; or you might want to work in conjunction with a specific publisher to create a bespoke piece of native content – written in the publication's style and tone of voice – that conveys the information you want to get across accurately. Or you could do both – and 20 other variations of the same – and split-test what content and what delivery mechanism works for the best results.

CASE STUDY Brand content: Villas.com and *The Independent*

Villas.com wanted to raise awareness of its website among young professionals and families, highlighting the range of properties available and the benefits of rentals versus traditional hotel breaks.

Solutions

To inspire readers with the range of Villas.com properties and the benefits of self-catering versus a hotel experience, *The Independent* created first-hand accounts of holidays that would appeal to the different target groups. They sent writers on a weekend break to Venice with an off-grid itinerary for food-lovers, plus a family-and-friends weekend closer to home in Suffolk. In addition, they created a fun graphical guide on indy100 with practical tips for taking great holiday photos and correcting the not-so-good ones. Alongside this, they ran a competition in print and on digital for a chance to win £10,000 when users shared their best holiday snaps.

Results

While the campaign consisted of only three pieces of content, it generated more than 50,000 page views, more than twice the anticipated level. The Suffolk weekend article, which was the best-performing piece, attracted more than 20,000 page views – four times the average expected audience.

Why it worked

This is a good example of how, sometimes, keeping it simple works best. This campaign works because of its simplicity: the right content to the right audience. *The Independent* adopted an editorial approach to the brand content, creating informative content that the target audience would enjoy. Practical advice, combined with inspirational and aspirational content, led to the content over-performing in terms of audience reach. It works.

Build your brand personality

As mentioned above, one of the key benefits of native advertising is the ability to distribute different types of content, at scale. But another key benefit of native advertising is the ability to experiment and cultivate your brand tone of voice. For example, if you want to share the story of how your business was founded, or feature a personal story behind one of your team members, native advertising is the natural format to use to distribute this content – to reach and engage with your target audience. In the past brands would have had to try to reach audiences with this sort of content via banner ads – where engagement and click-through rates are minimal – and more often than not the criteria for success was sales or leads. But with native advertising, offering an effective distribution platform for these more personable stories – the behind-the-scenes-look, if you will, behind brand businesses – the reasons for not creating more of these stories diminishes for brands. As a brand looking to interrupt the feed of busy people going about their daily lives, you have to act personably – almost like a person – and, as we've already outlined in this book, that has to include a story. If you don't, you are just a commodity, interrupting their day. Get it right and your brand could be viewed as a trusted, valued 'friend'.

Experiment at scale, cheaply

One of the truly great things about native advertising is that as well as being able to run any sort of asset that you might have at your disposal in terms of content, the scale and reach you can achieve with native advertising as a medium is largely unequalled. You can experiment at scale using native advertising like no other ad format. Facebook, which pioneered many native advertising formats and only runs native ad formats across its platform, had 1.18 billion daily active users on average in September 2016;[3] Outbrain, a leading content recommendation provider, reaches a global audience of over 557 million each month.[4] On a smaller scale, my business, ADYOULIKE, serves in excess of 5 billion native ads each month across publishers in the US, UK, France and many other global markets. The ability to run billions and billions of ads – targeting millions of consumers (if you so desire) – is easily achieved with native advertising.

Targeting

Obviously all but the largest of brands look to target millions upon millions of consumers with their advertising messages, but, with all of these available consumers at scale comes audience data that is almost unimaginable to fathom in terms of detail. For example, did you know that Facebook uses as many as 98 personal data points to target ads to its members,[5] making the targeting functionality of the social network so effective? This is why you often receive super-relevant ads direct in your Facebook feed.

There's no denying the effectiveness of this data for marketers looking to target relevant audiences. Remember the mantra from earlier in the book: right person, right place, right time – Facebook advertising gets advertisers close to this, arguably more often than any other medium.

Where Facebook leads, the market has followed. So it's not just Facebook that has this capability. All other social media platforms hold similar levels of data and targeting capability. In-feed native programmatic technologies, which run billions of native ads each month, have increasingly complex targeting capabilities based on user data and artificial intelligence (AI) (there's more on AI in Chapter 16, The Next Generation of Native Advertising). Likewise, all major publishers worth their salt have recognized the value of data to their businesses and have built up sophisticated data and targeting capabilities as a result. The level of granular targeting that modern advertisers can achieve with native advertising is unparalleled.

Retargeting

Another way native advertising can help achieve your business objectives is through retargeting. Retargeting, or remarketing as it is also termed, essentially lets you retarget your ad messages to website visitors who haven't already converted. Sophisticated algorithms and user data effectively combine to give you a second bite of the cherry when it comes to targeting would-be buyers of your product or services. You can target shoppers who have visited your site, but not bought, or even target those who may have seen your advertising somewhere once already, with additional messaging. Cross-channel remarketing is a major opportunity for advertisers. Simply, this means that you retarget your customers across all of your marketing channels. So if someone clicks on your Google Ad Words ad, you retarget them via a Facebook ad, or if someone clicks on your Facebook ad, you retarget them via in-feed native advertising placements on premium publishers.

The opportunities are endless, and as native advertising is engaged with far more than traditional display advertising, the performance of native advertising when combined with retargeting is significant.

What type of native advertising should you try out for your business?

Below we will outline in a little more detail how native advertising can work for your business type; we'll also offer recommendations on what type of native advertising products you may want to test and find out more about. The recommendations below are largely based on performance, but as much as anything on price, too: I don't see the point in recommending a native product that could cost an SME a significant amount of money, with a variable degree of return on investment. A point to note, though: no one knows your business, your budgets and your core audience and performance objectives better than you – what works for your competitor, you may see as underperformance, and vice versa. So read on and decide for yourself.

Brand advertisers

The benefits to big brand advertisers that native advertising offers have been well documented. There are many advantages that native advertising has over other forms of digital advertising – and the benefits to big brands are similar to the benefits that all other advertisers will see. As outlined above, the fact that native advertising is the default distribution model for brand content means that any big brand should be heavily invested in all facets of native advertising. There really is no reason why a brand should not be looking to use all available consumer touch points, layering on data, while widening their scale, to engage their target audience in the feed, as they congregate around the 'collective camp fire'.

Recommended native products: all of them.

SME businesses

There are many opportunities for SMEs in using native advertising. As outlined above, the level of data and targeting are unbeatable, while the option to scale where relevant means that it's possible for SME businesses to harness the power of native advertising to grow their brand presence and share their brand personality to a relevant audience in an affordable way. It is genuinely possible to use native advertising across all of a customer sales cycle – for prospecting, product research, closing deals, repeat purchase, ongoing customer service operations and more.

Do-it-yourself native advertising

It's easy to get confused and muddled up with different opportunities and what messages to place where; hopefully this book will help you understand the processes and the opportunity that native advertising affords in more detail. But if you are an SME and you are looking to significantly scale your native advertising approach, recruiting the services of an agency – with proven content marketing and native advertising credentials – would likely generate better results than going solo. It should save you worrying about losing any money by making expensive mistakes.

In terms of what native products to use, this will largely come down to your overall budget, as well as your particular industry or niche. All products could work, but there are probably a few mainstays. Social media advertising is relatively inexpensive – and can be highly targeted – so is worth running. Facebook and Twitter are worth reviewing; whether you decide to opt for LinkedIn, too, will depend on whether you are a B2B (business-to-business) business or not. Likewise, platforms such as Snapchat and Instagram may be worth exploring depending on your target audience.

Content recommendation units are equally affordable and are good for driving traffic to your website, while in-feed units across premium publishers, particularly when purchased on a cost-per-click basis, may also be worth considering. Depending on your product or service, partnering with one specific publisher to create brand content in the publisher's tone of voice may be a possibility. This can be an expensive option, however, as publishers typically charge a premium for this type of content creation and for allowing brands access to their audiences in the tone of voice of their publication. But it can work, particularly for B2B businesses, or those businesses targeting niche consumer groups. For example, if you are a B2B business that sells wall tiles to builders, a native partnership with a leading B2B building trade magazine makes sense. Likewise, if you are a company that sells mountain climbing equipment, a partnership with the leading mountain climbing publication in your market makes sense, too.

Recommended native ad products: all of them.

Start-ups

Unless you are a well-funded, venture-capital-backed start-up with money to burn, the objectives of start-ups in the very early days tend to be quite similar to those of SMEs – just with less money to lose. A key concern is: 'how do I grow, without wasting my money?' Experimenting with digital marketing can be expensive, but also damaging if done badly, for a fledgling, boot-strapped start-up business. But as a start-up, you cannot fail to act – you have to do something with your digital advertising budget if you want to grow. So what do you do? Take it slowly. Experiment. Test, test and test again. All start-ups will be familiar with making less go further – and this is never more important than with your advertising budget. It's easy to create and run many multiples of content headlines and different types of content and scale up slowly with native. Make sure you pay particular attention to the headlines you run.

Remember, too, what we said about targeting and scale: the more you can experiment and learn now in your start-up phase, the more valuable insights you'll have for future marketing efforts, as you'll know what works and what doesn't. This will be invaluable as you grow – get it right and you can grow your market share to unimaginable scale, quickly.

Like SMEs, running native ads with social media platforms makes sense, as well as content recommendation units.

Native advertising products for start-ups

On a limited budget it might be prudent to stay away from publisher brand content campaigns – as you are looking for flexibility to test across large platforms until you know what works really well for you. Only buy native advertising on a cost-per-click (CPC) basis; that way you only pay for performance. Look at your targeting and retargeting options, alongside your brand messaging, and then look at all available options a few months in. Also, if budget allows, recruit the services of an agency, or a specialist freelancer, to help run and manage this activity for you: managing your advertising can be a costly distraction and, if this is an area you are unfamiliar with, get an expert in – so you can concentrate on doing what you do best and running your busy start-up.

Recommended native ad products: CPC native advertising to start, content recommendation, social advertising, in-feed native.

The power of native advertising on brand uplift

Pergo is one of the largest US floor manufacturers. In 2015 Pergo were looking to increase brand awareness around their hardwood floors. Pergo teamed up with TripleLift, a native advertising platform specializing in in-feed and programmatic native advertising. In addition, Nielsen Digital Brand Effect was utilized to help further understand the impact of their native advertising efforts on raising awareness of the Pergo brand.

Nielsen Digital Brand Effect measures digital brand advertising performance in real time. This allows marketers to measure the performance of key elements driving brand uplift, such as creative, targeting and frequency, and make optimizations while the campaign is still running.

Optimizations based on the findings reported in the Nielsen Digital Brand Effect dashboard by TripleLift during the campaign increased Pergo brand uplift by 36.8%.[6]

Native advertising and search engine optimization

When native advertising first became popular as a term, there were many in the SEO (search engine optimization) business who looked at it purely as a vehicle to help improve the search results of their websites and clients. All the other benefits of native advertising were inconsequential to them. For SEO experts, anything that can generate some high-quality do-follow backlinks, increase page views and extra social shares, is worthwhile. Why? Because these factors will have a major impact on search results for a website. The majority of SEOs use native advertising to their advantage in a number of ways.

Generating backlinks with native advertising

If you are not familiar with SEO, one of the key ways to increase your positioning in search engines is to generate links to your website from website search engines. For example, a link from a publication like the *New York*

Times, the *Guardian*, *Le Figaro* or the BBC direct to your website is seen as a big thumbs-up for your website and its contents to search engines.

The majority of native advertising created and hosted by premium publishers today will link back to the advertisers' website at some point within the copy, but increasingly those backlinks are deemed 'no-follow'.

What does no-follow mean? The clue is in the name: it's effectively an instruction to search engine spiders to not follow the link and not include it as a backlink to this site. In layman's terms, it's taking away the thumbs-up.

Without going deep into the SEO rabbit hole (and believe me, it goes way, way deep), some SEOs believe that backlinks, whether no-follow or not, still add considerable weight to search results. And they could well be right. But whether no-follow or otherwise, SEOs benefit from using native advertising to help generate backlinks. They also use native advertising in other ways to help achieve their aim of improving organic search engine results. In summary, these are:

- **Driving traffic to site:** while backlinks are an important factor in SEO, another key indicator that search engines increasingly look at is the number of visits those pages receive. It makes sense, I suppose. In theory, you could assume that the higher the number of visits a particular page has, the more relevant the content on that page is, therefore it's worth a search engine bumping this page up the listings. Increasingly these factors contribute – especially when combined with markers such as dwell time (how long each user spends on a page) and bounce rate (whether or not the site visitor clicks through to other areas of a site, or they hit back to the search results during a session) – to give search engines a view of whether or not a page should be ranked highly or not.

- **Increasing social shares:** in conjunction with the above, social shares are another key factor that search engines take on board in determining the relevancy and popularity of pages. The more shares a page has, the higher the metaphorical thumbs-up.

- **Boosting backlink content pages:** while SEOs use native advertising to promote traffic with the aim of driving relevant users to their site – hopefully to increase metrics such as visits, dwell time and social shares – another popular tactic used by SEOs (and you can too) is to use native advertising to drive traffic to other pages that sit outside of your website domain, but that may link through to your website. Why do they do this? The simple answer is that good SEOs not only look to boost the traffic, performance and search engine results of their destination websites, but they also look to do so for good-quality pages that link back to their client site. They look to raise the status of all, or many, pages that link to their own website, safe in the knowledge that if all of these pages receive a bump up the search results pages from the likes of Google, their website is likely to benefit too. Confusing, I know, but increasingly it is native advertising that is being used to help drive this up for SEOs.

Let's look at an example:

My website: I launch my new website dalesnativeadvertisingbook.com. Within a week the website is referenced and linked to via three ad industry blog posts published on three separate blogs. As an SEO I am already using native advertising to drive traffic directly through to dalesnativeadvertisingbook. com – remember, I'm looking to increase traffic to my site to gain a better search ranking position. The more traffic, shares, dwell time and bounce rate I have, the better my quality score will be and I'll move up the rankings. But now I've seen these three new links come into my site from three favourable websites, writing favourable articles about my website. So if I'm a clever SEO I now have an idea. I could improve my chances of moving up in search results even more if I also drive traffic to those articles – as I know that the more traffic, shares, dwell time and better bounce rate I can generate for these pages, the better the quality score this page will receive, moving it up the rankings. The higher these pages are, the bigger the thumbs-up from search engines when they see a link from it to my site. So by boosting the score of these pages, I boost my own page's too – the better my quality score will be and I'll move up the rankings. Effectively all pages will move up the rankings together.

To some extent this is another example of creative SEOs using all available tools to gain the system and take a competitive advantage over their rivals. It's not necessarily using native advertising for its intended purpose. But it does work.

Put in another context, if you stand back and look at what SEOs do with native advertising, all they are doing is using native advertising to put good content in front of relevant people. They are still largely following the 'right people, right place, right time' mantra, albeit for different reasons. Whereas most marketers are using native advertising to reach audience and people, SEOs are using native advertising to target people, but with the end goal of improving a search engine result.

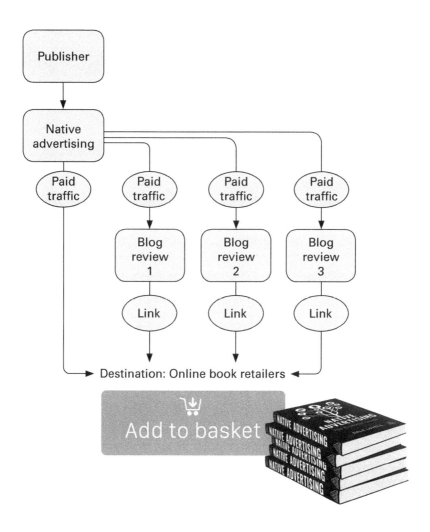

Affiliates

The affiliate marketing industry is huge. E-commerce has become part of everyday life – and increasingly becomes the normal way of buying all sorts of goods and services. Data from Adobe Insights, published in January 2017, showed that a momentous $91.7 billion was spent in the US alone via e-commerce over the 2016 holiday season from 1 November through to 31

December 2016.[7] This impressive figure is perhaps only topped by the fact that this amounted to an astonishing increase of 11 per cent from 2015. As e-commerce has become ubiquitous, affiliate schemes have flourished.

A study undertaken by Forrester Consulting on behalf of one of the world's largest affiliate networks found that the affiliate marketing space has matured into a significant channel for driving sales for advertisers of all sizes. US affiliate marketing spend is estimated to increase by a compound annual growth rate (CAGR) of 10.1 per cent between 2015 and 2020, to an estimated $6.8 billion industry. The study found that over 80 per cent of advertisers and 84 per cent of publishers surveyed ran an affiliate programme. In addition, more than 80 per cent of advertisers devoted over 10 per cent of their marketing budget to affiliate marketing.[8]

Affiliate marketing is big business. Not all affiliate marketers are fully utilizing the opportunity available to them with native advertising. They often only really use native advertising as a tool to boost their overall SEO, not as a performance driver. Native advertising is mentioned often as a great brand tool. Native campaigns are great for building brand awareness. But less is mentioned about the ability of native advertising to play a significant part in direct response campaigns – campaigns where the KPI is always sales, lead generation and your success or failure depends on hitting a cost per acquisition (CPA) target. For affiliates, it's always about CPA, and making a quantifiable return on investment.

It is a success that is often difficult to achieve. But native advertising is proven to work for these types of advertisers too. They work. Why? Because content can be persuasive. I recently ran a campaign for a leading female fashion brand that had a 200 per cent conversion ROI with a corresponding 42 per cent decrease in cost per sale. Native advertising works for direct sale.

Good content, distributed to the right audience, at the right time, on any device, can be very persuasive indeed. Remember: right person, right product, right time.

Even when the main campaign considerations are branding, native ads can still deliver sizeable sales. By being less annoying, advertising that adds value to a consumer generates better results – be it for brand or direct response. It's that simple. It's why native advertising works.

Native advertising and the PR industry

Even though native advertising has been popular for a number of years, I am still genuinely surprised at how slow the public relations (PR) sector has been to fully embrace native advertising. While the SEO industry is quick to pounce on any new tool or product that can provide first-mover advantage, the PR industry moves far more slowly.

As a sector the PR industry is undergoing enormous changes, almost as much as publishing itself. It's worth remembering that PR as an industry was largely built on getting coverage, more often than not, in daily newspapers with massive circulation figures. These publications are either no more, or are dwindling into obscurity: clients want more exposure digitally, and they expect their PRs to do more for them. Increasingly, a successful PR campaign revolves around exposure to the feed and telling stories around the 'collective campfire'.

So the fit, in my mind, between PR and native advertising is obvious. For a start, the PR industry has the talent. The PR industry, more than any other media sector, is full of storytellers – many PRs start their professional careers as journalists. This may have changed in recent years as PR has become increasingly a first-career choice among graduates, but senior figures at PR agencies worldwide know the power of content. The jump from crafting stories via PR distribution to story-based advertising is a small one.

Second, every PR team I've ever worked with instinctively has the trust of their clients when it comes to content and content strategy. They write a lot of great content and it's often the PR agency that clients turn to for feedback on content, not, for example, their media agency.

PRs understand content and often immerse themselves in their client's products and services to a far higher degree than other agencies are required to – which means they're exceptionally well placed to create and offer native-based content marketing campaigns.

PRs are well placed to sell in native solutions

So selling native into clients appears, on the surface, to be simple for PR. After all, the majority of PR businesses already run native advertising via paid-for posts on Facebook and promoted tweets on Twitter. Few do much else.

In fact, in a bid to help highlight the issue to the UK PR industry, at ADYOULIKE we commissioned a survey among PR agencies in January 2016 on the topic of native advertising. The result revealed that 88 per cent of UK PRs surveyed admitted they saw native advertising as an opportunity for the sector, while 75 per cent believed they should be the best choice to create and distribute native advertising content for brands.[9]

Since this study was published, very little has changed. The only native advertising the vast majority of PR agencies undertake currently is paid social media posts – our survey found that 63 per cent of PRs use paid methods to boost Twitter and Facebook ads.

Native advertising is actually a tool with enormous potential for the PR sector, as it allows agencies to offer reach and scale to their clients in a way that simply wasn't possible before. Native advertising enables PR agencies to take their ideas further and deepen the relationship they have with their clients. It allows PRs to extend the content they've developed for those brands and share it beyond just that first piece of editorial – either on social networks or via premium publisher environments.

An article in a print magazine or national newspaper can't really be used elsewhere, but a great piece of online coverage (or content on their own or clients' websites) can be distributed via native advertising to other publishers that target similar key audiences, increasing the reach and value of that content for a brand. In short, native advertising is a great way to extend the reach of positive PR coverage through paid-for media. It is also a great way to establish an 'always-on' strategy that generates true engagement and weds together a brand's activity around social media, PR, display and content into one integrated, holistic strategy with easily identifiable ROI.

Of course, there are some challenges. Many PRs (and their clients) are put off by the word 'advertising' in native advertising. They find that hard to sell in to their clients.

Start-up PR tip – maximizing exposure with native ads

A great tip for content recommendation units that I think many start-ups miss is using content recommendation units to amplify their start-up PR. Let me explain.

It's common for many start-ups to invest in some launch PR activity; it's normally for a limited period of time, though, and it tends to generate mixed levels of success. If this is you and you can generate at least one good bit of PR around your product or launch, I would use it to run in your content recommendation campaign. It can help amplify your PR reach to your right audience.

For example, when a mid-market Midwestern newspaper ran an interview with an expert supporting their client's stance on an important policy debate, PR firm Fleishman-Hillard – a top global communications firm that specializes in public relations, public affairs, marketing, paid media, transmedia, and social content – used Outbrain to drive traffic to the story. The result: they ended up netting an additional placement in the process. A *Huffington Post* writer saw it and picked up the story shortly after Fleishman-Hillard started their Outbrain campaign.

This is just one example of how you can use content and native advertising to tie into your wider marketing and business objectives.

Blurred lines

Some communication and PR professionals will have concerns around the 'blurred lines' of editorial and advertising that native advertising has supposedly created. The blurred lines between journalism and PR have been in place for a generation or more. Much of what we read in the press is not journalism; rather, it's 'churnilism' – marketing press releases from newswires passed off as editorial content. Not all of it is fact-checked by cash-strapped, time-poor publishers. As a consumer, I feel more comfortable reading content that is clearly labelled as 'advertising', but informative on a particular topic, than something that is taken almost verbatim from a marketing press release but published as impartial journalism under the guise of editorial. How about you?

The fact of the matter is that the digital revolution has blurred the lines in terms of agency responsibility: media buyers create content now; PR agencies buy media. It's a situation that is not going to go away. The PR sector needs to adapt to it.

For the PR sector, native advertising offers a way into entirely new brand budgets, as well as a way to show off and flex their creative muscles in a digital environment not dissimilar to the media world they already know so intimately.

So if you do work in PR, congratulations: the fact you are reading this books means that you recognize the opportunity, too.

Who can benefit summary

The key to success with native advertising, as with other forms of advertising, is to experiment. The great thing about native advertising is that there are multiple ways to experiment without breaking the bank. From big name brands down to solo enterprises, there's a native product available that is right for you. Follow the rest of the tips within this book, reach out to the relevant native advertising providers, test and learn to see what works for your business. The native advertising opportunity really is worth the effort of investing – and if you aren't looking at it, you can bet your competitors are.

Endnotes

1 AOP (4 March 2015) AOP releases The Power of Native research report [online] www.ukaop.org/aop-news/aop-news/aop-releases-the-power-of-native-research-report [accessed 28 March 2017]

2 Smart Insights (2017) Display Ad CTR benchmarks – March 2017 update [online] www.smartinsights.com/internet-advertising/internet-advertising-analytics/display-advertising-clickthrough-rates/ [accessed 28 March 2017]

3 Facebook (2017) Company Information Page [online] http://newsroom.fb.com/company-info/ [accessed 28 March 2017]

4 Outbrain (2017) Available at: www.outbrain.com/amplify [accessed 28 March 2017]

5 Dewey, C (19 August 2016) 98 personal data points that Facebook uses to target ads to you, *Washington Post* [online] www.washingtonpost.com/news/the-intersect/wp/2016/08/19/98-personal-data-points-that-facebook-uses-to-target-ads-to-you/ [accessed 28 March 2017]

6 Nielsen (2015) Building brand lift from the ground up [online] www.nielsen.com/content/dam/corporate/us/en/reports-downloads/2015-reports/dbe-pergo-triplelift-case-study.pdf [accessed 28 March 2017]

7 Abramovich, G (17 January 2017) ADI: Holiday 2016 unwraps new online shopping behaviors [online] www.cmo.com/adobe-digital-insights/articles/2017/1/13/adi-holiday-2016-recap-report.html [accessed 28 March 2017]

8 mThink (4 February 2016) Affiliate marketing industry to grow to $6.8 billion over next five years [online] http://mthink.com/affiliate-marketing-industry-grow-6-8-billion-next-five-years/ [accessed 28 March 2017]

9 ADYOULIKE (17 February 2016) Nine out of ten PR agencies see native advertising as an opportunity [online] www.prnewswire.co.uk/news-releases/nine-out-of-ten-pr-agencies-see-native-advertising-as-an-opportunity-569115771.html [accessed 28 March 2017]

Measuring native advertising: does it work?

In this chapter we are going to look at the effectiveness of native advertising. We are going to showcase some case study examples of native advertising – and the reach it can generate. We'll look at how and with what tools native advertising is being measured today, and we'll also look at the debate that exists around the measurement of content-led advertising. We'll hear from experts in the field and ask the question: do we need to set a new measurement metric for native advertising?

The first steps to success

To succeed with native advertising, you first need to know what 'success' actually looks like. What is the metric you are going to use to determine whether or not your native advertising is a success?

For the majority of native advertising campaigns that are run, key performance indicators (KPIs) typically fall into one or more of the below, which we'll run through in more detail:

- **Visits:** rightly or wrongly, for many advertisers the number one criterion for success when they run native advertising campaigns is, 'How many visits did it bring to my site?'

- **Dwell time and bounce rate:** these two KPIs often go hand in hand with visits as a measure of success. Dwell time is the measure of how long a visitor spends on a specific page – so can be used, in a slightly crude fashion, as an indicator of whether someone read and enjoyed the content on the page. Bounce rate, which is a key search metric, is the indication of what the user did after landing on the page: did they click back or close the window, or was their interest piqued enough by this page to move along to other pages on the site? Both are metrics used to understand the 'stickiness' of content and websites, and to tell if visitors enjoy these pages.

- **Click-through rate:** a common metric of success, based on how many clicks your advertising gets.

- **Engagement:** this is a similar KPI to dwell time, but the process of measurement is very different. While dwell time is typically measured on the advertiser's website, usually via Google Analytics, engagement is a metric that is usually measured via a publisher, native technology platform or other third-party advertising tracking. What does it mean? It is a measure of how long someone 'engaged' with your content. This could be how long, on average, did someone spend reading your publisher partnership brand content published on BuzzFeed, Mashable or the LADbible? Or it could be the average length of time someone spent watching your brand video, which ran across multiple premium publishers via in-feed distribution technologies such as Sharethrough, TripleLift or ADYOULIKE.

- **Shares and likes:** for many advertisers, native advertising is a tool to be used to generate shares of their content and likes for their pages. This is particularly the case, though not exclusively, with social media advertising. For many advertisers using social media advertising, they are looking for as many shares of their content as possible – shares that hopefully translate into lots of likes for their social media profiles, and more visitors to their site. But ultimately shares equal extended reach for your brand's marketing messages and increases the available pool of relevant customers you can engage with at any point in the future.

- **Sales and leads:** while 'soft' metrics such as engagement and visits are very popular measures of success, native advertising is increasingly being used as a pure direct response marketing channel. For these advertisers, success is easy to quantify: did I create any sales leads, or did I manage to generate any sales as a result of this native advertising? Sophisticated advertisers increasingly use native advertising in conjunction with other forms of digital advertising for strong sales results. When combined with data, retargeting, cookies and attribution modelling, native advertising is a growing part of the modern sales lead marketing mix.

A publisher's view on native advertising KPIs

Contributed by Kolja Kleist, Director, Customer and Brand Management

Burda Forward is one of the leading digital publishers in Germany responsible for Germany's largest news publication (www.focus.de) and largest digital lifestyle portal (chip.de).

At Burda Forward we measure KPIs such as visits, dwell time, engagement, shares, leads and sales, but we also track even more – such as scroll depth. It depends on what is really important for the client. We have our own realtime dashboard with 'live link' for our clients. We tried to figure out what KPIs are really relevant for which phase of the customer journey (awareness, consideration and action). What will be very important in the future is to give an answer on how to compare native advertising with classic stuff such as display and video. This is still very hard for media agencies and clients to measure.

There are other KPIs in existence, but the above are the main metrics currently popular with advertisers and publishers. Some publishers, such as the *Financial Times* in the UK, have trialled selling advertisers on a time-per-hour metric, similar to dwell time. Many advertisers also have their own measurement criteria, based on sophisticated performance data, impressions, clicks, sales generated and purchase intent, that they use to analyse all of their digital marketing activity, not just native advertising. But the native advertising market is currently largely based around the above listed KPIs.

A crucial question to ask yourself before you even think about running a native advertising campaign is: what does success look like to you? If social shares are meaningless for your business goals, or visitors to your website is the only thing you care about, this will obviously influence what type of native advertising you ultimately choose to run. Think about it first, then choose a native ad product – not the other way around.

Tracking advertiser performance

The great thing about digital advertising is that almost everything can be tracked. It's possible to track all clicks and impressions on your advertising, with the ability to break down what advertising ran where and by whom. You can access more data than you will know what to do with, if you want it, that is.

Tracking is key if you want to gauge how well your advertising is running. If, for example, you are using two, three or four different advertising partners at the same time, promoting the same activity, how are you going to know which ones are performing best if you are not tracking it individually?

The same is true for different types of content that you are running. If it's not set up to be tracked, you are missing out on a substantial amount of data and information that can be used to cut advertising spend waste, but also to substantially grow the performance of your advertising – performance that can easily be translated back to increased revenue for your business. So don't even think about running any sort of digital advertising – not just native advertising – without sorting out the tracking that you have in place first.

Tracking the performance of your native advertising

There are numerous ways to track the performance of your native advertising. There are sophisticated third-party tracking tools that are used for all digital advertising. These allow you to create tags that can be inputted and supplied to your native ad partners as third-party verification that your advertising is being served to the volume you've booked and in the correct manner. If you are going to invest a significant amount of money on digital advertising, I recommend that you look into these businesses and their pricing models in more detail, as failure to have proper tracking set up leaves you vulnerable to poor performance. Check out DoubleClick, Sizmek and Atlas.

Measuring native advertising with Google Analytics

A number of SME businesses, as well as those purely measuring the success or failure of their campaigns based on website visitor metrics and how long those visitors interact with their website, often simply measure success against their Google Analytics tools.

We will not go into too much detail here about Google Analytics (GA), but GA is the default tool used by the vast majority of publishers globally to analyse their website visitors, traffic sources, dwell time and more. It's the tool used to determine if one piece of content is more successful than another. It monitors shares, time on the page, bounce rate, geographic location of a website visitor, device and operating system used to access the content, and a whole lot more.

Many publishers and advertisers looking to set up and run their own native advertising campaigns often rely on what are called UTM links. UTM stands for Urchin Tracking Module, after the company Urchin Software Corporation, which was purchased by Google in 2005. UTM is a key component of Google Analytics. Essentially, a UTM code is a bit of extra text that publishers and advertisers – and you – can add to a website link that then provides Google Analytics with a little bit more information about the link. An example looks like this:

utm_source=adyoulike&utm_medium=native&utm_campaign=sale

UTM code allows you to split up and identify traffic sources to the same page more easily. It lets you:

- see where your website traffic is coming from: source=adyoulike;
- see which type of product is sending you this traffic: medium=native;
- see which campaign is sending you traffic: campaign=sale.

It then allows you to break down the performance of this traffic in ever more detail. So it's possible to analyse the performance of each partner, advertiser, publisher, or social media site, like for like, against others.

The problem in using Google Analytics to measure advertising

Google Analytics is a superb, sophisticated tool that millions of publishing professionals use day in, day out. I've used it extensively myself and it's seriously impressive, which you'd expect from Google. But when it comes to using GA for monitoring digital advertising performance – and the performance of native advertising in promoting content in particular – there are some big issues. Why? Currently thousands of advertisers are using GA incorrectly for the purpose of measuring their advertising performance.

The majority of content marketers measure visits, dwell time and bounce rate via Google Analytics. But anyone using Google Analytics as a referrer visit counter – that is, to see where visits come from – is likely to run into data discrepancies. Without getting bogged down in the technicalities at play, the main issue is in reporting methodologies.

DoubleClick Support advises that clients do not try to reconcile Google Analytics data with Desktop for Publishers (DFP) reporting. The Australian Designalicious.com blog explains the reasoning:

> A discrepancy between DoubleClick and analytics is to be expected because of the standing differences in reporting methodologies; DoubleClick data is based on ad server logs and it is generally much more accurate at reporting ad impressions than analytics data, which is based on cookies or page loads.[1]

The main reasons for discrepancies between Google Analytics and ad servers are:

- different counting methodologies (server-based counting versus counting cookies or page loads);
- not counting the same thing: a click with an advertiser is not the same as an impression in analytics packages.

Comparing referrer URLs to advertiser clicks is bad practice, as referrers in Google Analytics aren't an accurate measure of clicks or landings for the following reasons:

- Referrers can be disabled on most browsers.
- Internet security applications can block referrer data.
- Firewall and proxy servers can filter out referrers.
- Users can set up referrer spoofing to prevent a site from knowing where they've been.
- Depending on the ad type (rich media, standard image, etc) and the ad tag (iFrame, JavaScript, standard HTML etc) on the page, the referrer can often simply be changed from that of your advertiser traffic source to come through simply as either DoubleClick or 'your site'.

iFrames

A number of publishers run their advertising through iFrames. iFrames are essentially a way to display a webpage within another webpage. Publishers like iFrames in many instances because it gives them greater control over advertiser code. Many native advertising placements run through iFrames. They are very common ways to integrate and serve advertising. But this has major issues with Google Analytics.

With many devices and browsers, the referrer URL is not provided via iFrame and the origin of the user is often listed as 'blank'. In this case, for example, a user who clicked on an iFrame ad would be, on the landing page, considered as having typed in the URL directly in the browser and analytics would not record the user as originating from another website or source. It would therefore not display your partner or traffic source as a referrer in your analytics.

In addition, many browsers directing traffic through iFrames are set to block third-party cookies; they will block the Google Analytics cookies and Google Analytics won't work in terms of a referrer.[2]

Why does this Google Analytics issue matter?

This matters for a number of reasons. To start with, it leaves many native advertising campaigns being judged as successful or not on inaccurate data. The performance of a campaign is being judged on data that is appearing inaccurately on a platform not designed to measure the activity that is being recorded. This is potentially damaging for native advertising's reputation. It's like running an election and declaring a winner when you know you've failed to count a large proportion of the votes cast. Or like running an election, failing to tell half the electorate the day of the election, and failing to count a large swathe of the votes cast after closing the polls too. It's a data nightmare.

It can be costly, too: for you, for your brand, everyone. How do you know if something works or not if you are measuring the wrong data, using the wrong tools? You might be dismissing a fantastic new marketing channel simply because your data is not speaking to you correctly. If this is you and your business currently: review what you are doing and what constitutes success.

What should native advertising be measuring?

There is a wider issue at play, of course – and one that sits at the very heart of native advertising. What are we measuring? For many content marketers adopting native advertising, success or failure is gauged via Google Analytics. Whether the data is skewed or not is beside the point for many of them. If Google Analytics says so, it is. That's all they care about. But for traditional display advertisers adopting native advertising, Google Analytics performance is often a secondary, or third, consideration. These advertisers care far more about brand uplift, purchase intent, sales and leads. Likewise, other advertisers look for content shares on social media as a criterion for success.

There's no one-size-fits-all approach. Again, this is testament to the fact that native advertising can be 'all things to all people', which means that it is judged by different criteria from campaign to campaign. But should it be this way?

Does native advertising need a new measurement metric?

From brand to brand, publisher to publisher, different measurement criteria seem to apply. What constitutes a successful native campaign? There exists no consistent measurement for native advertising in its current form. But adopting a universal measurement has its challenges. The unique appeal of native advertising as something that does not quite fit into standardized advertising models does not easily lend itself to a universal measurement metric.

Measuring content performance

The first challenge is content itself. One of the major challenges around measuring content and thereby native advertising is that content can and does play a role through the entire customer sales cycle. So comparing like-for-like content on a single measurement such as sales leads or click-through rates can be problematic. Content that works for generating leads may be terrible for keeping existing customers engaged, and vice versa.

It is even tougher when you think that native advertising encompasses a range of formats: long- and short-form written editorial (some held within the publisher and some driven off-site), and images and video, all of which can have their own separate measurement metrics too.

Little wonder, then, that native advertising is sold in a number of different ways. Historically publishers have tended to sell their content and native advertising on a fixed-price tenancy, but this does seem to be changing to more CPM (cost per mille), CPC (cost per click) and CPE (cost per engagement) models – pricing models taken from traditional print publishing, digital display and video advertising. Are these the best for native?

The issue currently is that the different ways of selling create an environment where clicks and impressions become the default measurement of success for native ad campaigns because there is a monetary value attributed to them. We are some way off any sort of uniformity on establishing a content trading currency.

The challenge of measuring content and native advertising

Contributed by Clare O'Brien, former Head of Industry Programmes, IAB UK

The onset of native and content-based advertising solutions has presented the industry with a complex challenge. How do we establish meaningful and consistent measures that underpin the digital trading environment *and* allow the evaluation of campaign effectiveness?

Digital advertising is, despite its complicated trading structure, relatively simple in terms of how it's valued, which is essentially through a combination of impressions, clicks and views. The ecosystem is essentially based on *reach* data (viewable impressions or opportunities to see, CPM), or when publishers are rewarded by clicks (CPC), view-through rates (VCRs) or sales or leads acquired (CPAs). Commonly, clicks, VTRs, even social likes, etc, are used to evaluate campaign effectiveness: clicks equal *engagement*, or at least they used to.

So, it's a pretty blunt instrument and an inadequate framework to value, for example, publisher advertiser partnerships that create branded content and native advertising. Likewise, it doesn't take into account *context and environment*, say, or *attention* or *creative impact*, nor can it measure emotional response to and track changes in brand preference or propensity to buy. Critically, it doesn't even begin to address the intrinsic trust an audience has in a publisher brand – the impact of the media itself.

This is not to say that agencies, publishers and brands aren't urgently considering these issues. They are. At the time of writing, early 2017, measurement is one of the most important challenges across the industry. It's just that every constituent has a different stake in the eco-system. Finding industry-wide agreement is likely to be a long-running story in the development of a sustainable measurement framework for content and native – one where consistency allows the shared understanding of what advertiser/publisher partnerships look like and consist of, how the scale distribution of native ad units are valued, and one which provides advertisers with predictable returns.

The heart of the discussion is that 'content', across the breadth of its definitions (stuff that people want to engage with – watch or read, if you like) is both the creative ad and the medium. Because digital media is infinitely measureable, unlike its traditional predecessors, there is a widely held notion that it is possible to develop a criterion that measures both the effectiveness of the 'behaviour-changing' creative message, and the effectiveness of the media at placing that message in front of the people whose behaviour it is looking to change. This may be true, but the likelihood of creating a single algorithmically governed measure or trading unit will be wholly reliant on the entire eco-system accepting consistent measures which gather in more than digital's current reach and frequency scale metrics.

Some talk about a 'God metric', the possibility of a single algorithm that will be used to buy and sell media, evaluate campaign success and optimize the process. In a way, this idea is a distraction from the real problem, which is: how do we even understand what it is we're measuring and how can this be done reliably and consistently while delivering insight into all stages of the customer journey with all the digital tools at our fingertips – and those being developed?

The sheer diversity of the type of 'content' or 'native' outputs adds considerably to the challenge, with a rapidly expanding set of outputs being classed as 'content'. For example, journalism techniques that use video, audio, text and, say, animated graphics are content. So too are buy buttons, hyperlinks and XML-powered relational sign-ups, as well as how people react to these things. Putting aside whether a campaign is top or bottom of the funnel, the existence of this extraordinary smorgasbord of content types that may each play a different role in the customer journey with the brand needs widespread understanding, as do the means of measuring engagement and effectiveness.

In June 2016, the IAB UK's Content and Native Council published its *Measurement Green Paper*.[3] The idea was to help shape the industry conversation around consistent themes – it didn't establish how the challenge would be solved, rather it explored in some detail the extent of the challenge. It's a very useful reference to start considering your role in that conversation. Sixteen companies contributed their points of view, case studies, perspectives, opinions and learnings, as well as the likely direction of travel. Many of the points above were addressed.

If that paper has a conclusion, it was that there is much work to be done and there must be shared willingness of all participants – not least the brands – to be open and transparent with all data points for consistent, algorithmic measures and techniques to be developed. The point on which everyone was agreed is that current digital trading metrics are only a part of the solution and that, as with traditional media, there has to be investment in understanding how people behave with content-based and native advertising before establishing algorithms that measure those behaviours.

Conclusion

The challenge in adopting a new metric is that the number that publishers and advertisers have most concerned themselves with has always been clicks and impressions. As we've highlighted in this chapter, there is a lot of debate about what, if anything, a native advertising measure should even look like. There are a lot of options to choose, ranging anywhere from traditional view and click metrics through to engagement metrics around shares, dwell time, bounce rate and referrals.

Should native follow TV models of reach and frequency, something similar to gross rating points? Or should we look at the possibility of establishing a new 'relationship metric' for native, something that measures elements of all of the above – views, clicks, engagement and reach – to create a universal measure? This has its problems, too, of course, and immediately raises the question: how do you define and measure a digital relationship exactly?

Navigating a way through this landscape is a challenge but one that can, and will, be addressed by the industry as a whole in the near future. Just as native advertising has already torn up the rulebook around what a digital ad should look like, it is undoubtedly set to disrupt the way in which digital advertising as a whole will be bought, sold and measured in the future too. Establishing what that metric looks like is of course the real challenge.

CASE STUDY Brand content: the *Guardian* and Unilever

In 2014 Unilever set out ambitious plans to double the size of its business while reducing its environmental footprint and making a more positive social impact.[4]

In a ground-breaking partnership with Unilever, the *Guardian* launched the Live Better Challenge, what it referred to as a 'rallying cry to all, encouraging the adoption of sustainable living practices. Put simply, we challenged people to live better.'

A new community-led section of the *Guardian*, sponsored by Unilever's Project Sunlight, was launched showing how sustainable living 'can be easy'. Editorial content was created by the *Guardian* and their content studio Guardian Labs showcasing monthly Live Better challenges, which featured contributions from *Guardian* journalists such as Zoë Williams. In addition, a documentary series of 26 short films about community-led projects throughout the UK was created. A series of brand stories were also created that ran across print and digital featuring 13 Unilever brands. These brand content pieces put the brand at the heart of the story, but ensured they were in keeping with the overall campaign objectives. Titles included: 'Colman's: making mustard sustainable' and 'Unilever: making cleanliness – and now sustainable living – commonplace'.

Additional activity included the publication of sustainable living lesson plans for educators, which was distributed via the *Guardian*'s teacher network to 252,000 UK teachers.

Results

- 8.6 million *Guardian* website reach (3+ million unique users);
- 446,000 engagements – comments, shares, video plays, challenge sign-ups;

- 9.9 million social reach, 16,000 tweets;
- 261% increase in Unilever as a trust mark;
- 37% increase on pre-campaign brand conversations;
- 40% increase in awareness of Unilever Project Sunlight.

Aside from the brand uplift metrics, the campaign is also estimated to have led to the saving of 10 tonnes of food waste, inspiring millions to take real action and attempt ongoing change.

Why it worked

This is an excellent example of taking an idea and running with it. The campaign worked for a number of reasons, but crucially because the idea was very much aligned to the beliefs of the target audience. This was a campaign that *Guardian* readers were likely to back. It works because there was buy-in from across the organization: the newsroom, columnists and feature writers all played their part. Crucially, it's also evident that there was also buy-in from the brand. Unilever appear to have trusted the *Guardian* to do what they do best – engage their audience with relevant content and championing a cause. Twenty years ago this brief probably would have been met with a proposal for a few advertorials; today it's a multifaceted campaign with significant reach beyond the environs of the publication in which it was published. This is a great example of how, when brand and publisher are aligned, it's possible to create branded content solutions that transcend their commercial objections and simply deliver outstanding editorial experiences that add real-life value and foster significant change.

Endnotes

1 Designalicious (11 February 2015) Double Click vs Google Analytics discrepancies [online] www.designalicious.com.au/ad-serving/19-double-click-vs-google-analytics-discrepancies [accessed 28 March 2017]

2 DoubleClick for Publishers Help (2017) Available at: https://support.google.com/dfp_premium/answer/6160380?hl=en&ref_topic=6160381 [accessed 28 March 2017]

3 IAB UK (31 May 2016) IAB Content and Native Measurement Green Paper [online] https://iabuk.net/resources/white-papers/content-and-native-measurement-green-paper [accessed 19 May 2017]

4 The *Guardian* Labs (no date) Inspiring people to live more sustainable lives with Unilever [online] https://guardianlabs.theguardian.com/projects/the-unilever-live-better-challenge [accessed 28 March 2017]

PART THREE
A practical guide to running native advertising

Getting started with native advertising 09

Now that you understand more about the digital advertising market and the main categories of native advertising – and how each one can play a part in your overall digital marketing mix – it's time to take your first steps in running your very own native advertising campaign. How you go about this, who you partner with, whether you use an ad agency or manage it all direct, and what budget you spend will largely be influenced by your own internal business set-up.

What assets do you have?

Now that you know what success looks like, it's time to look at how you make it happen. The first thing to look at is your existing content assets. Depending on your business – and whether you have started any content marketing as a marketing strategy or not – you will either feel that you have lots of great content worth promoting via native advertising, or none at all. The reality is that for almost all businesses, it's somewhere in between.

If you have a veritable production line of content being published to your blog and social media pages daily, perhaps you will be spoiled for choice. But there are a few questions to ask, before committing budget.

Do we want to pay to promote this content?

It may be a good piece of content for your blog or website, but is it something that you really want to be promoting across the digital landscape? Is it a bit risky, a bit out there, or is it just a bit dull? Does the world need to know about your new product update via this rather dry blog post, for example? If you have doubts, the answer is no.

Is it good enough to have money spent promoting it?

This one is slightly different from the above. It might, for example, be a nice, interesting blog post someone within your business has written and published. It's a good blog post, but too brief, and lacking in some additional research: does it meet the standards you think it should as a piece of journalism, for example, that you would expect to read on a quality website? If the answer is no, should you pay to promote it, as is?

Does it fit in with your overall marketing message?

You have just, finally, been given a 10-second clip from last year's TV ad which ran. It's well made, on point and even won an award for the creative agency that made it. You know it will work well as a native advertising campaign. But there's just one issue: the brand messages included in it are three months out of date now. You know this is all going to be updated shortly and changed. What should you do? You know what to do: there's no way you should confuse your brand message just because you have good content to promote. Remember: the content you promote has to fit your brand message, otherwise even the best content ever created will be a failure.

Is the value exchange a good one for your audience?

If it's a piece of content for content's sake – distribution for the sake of distribution – you are at risk of doing more harm than good. As we've outlined in other chapters, the quality of the content you produce has to offer some value to your target audience. You cannot expect to be liked if you promote rubbish.

Is the content set up to fully maximize the KPIs you are looking to achieve?

This is a key question to ask. I see it time and time again with many of my clients: they fail to optimize properly their content for their desired KPI. A lot of this stems from clients not knowing what success looks like.

Take dwell time and bounce rate, for example. It's common for distributors of content to often be asked to promote pages that are super-thin on content that have few discernable call-to-actions, or related links, on the page to encourage visitors to move around their sites once they are there. When the campaign fails to meet the client's desired dwell time and bounce rate KPIs, it is native advertising that is seen as having failed, when the reality is that it's the client's failure to properly optimize their content and website that is the major culprit for failure. We can bring a horse to water, but we can't make it drink.

Is your content feed-ready?

One of the bugbears native advertising platforms, networks and publishers continually have are concerns around the available assets. Very often, when large brands are involved, the assets that are handed over to be distributed are nothing more than hand-me-downs from non-digital creative. What do we mean by this exactly? TV ads for running as in-feed native or social media, for example. The content is often poorly set up to shine on native platforms. It's almost destined to underperform from the start.

Media agency MediaCom recognized this issue in terms of digital creative assets and launched a new service, Feed Ready, specifically to address the problem. The service, which is run by MediaCom Beyond Advertising's creative team, optimizes content based on specific platform requirements, data insights and consumer content expectations.

This might include, for example, adding subtitles to appeal to users who watch video in their newsfeeds on mobile devices without sound, or cutting videos into different lengths to suit different environments.

MediaCom claim that when native advertisers are given platform-appropriate content, it can rather easily boost viewing time – from an average of 6 to 10 seconds on Facebook, for example. This is quantified as a fourfold boost in brand recall and a three-fold increase in purchase intent. Essentially, adding four seconds delivers a 40% increase in media value.[1]

Organic performance of existing content

Before you commit any money towards marketing existing content assets, look at how this content has performed prior to the addition of any media spend. For example, you run a diet website and have two very similar blog posts that you think you would like to promote via native advertising. The first one is entitled *51 Ways to Lose Weight This Year*, the second *Weight Loss Tips Made Easy*. You know that the content of both is very similar.

They should both perform equally well, shouldn't they? Possibly. But before you decide to run a native ad campaign promoting these two articles, you decide to check your internal stats. You shared both on your Facebook page.

When you look at the stats you are surprised: the *51 Ways to Lose Weight This Year* post received five times the number of views, likes and shares as the other one. The results are similar when you look at your Google Analytics results, too. So which one should you run? What on the surface may seem to be similar pieces of content, when you dive into the data, often tells a different story.

Top Tip: always look at the popularity of your existing content and how it performs organically (with no paid media behind it) in order to gauge whether or not it will resonate when you add some paid media to it. The likelihood is that if something is popular with no paid media behind it, when it receives a boost via paid native advertising methods, it will continue to perform well.

This doesn't mean that you shouldn't experiment with different types of content, of course – often all an existing piece of content needs is a 'refresh' and optimizations around the title and description needed for it to appeal to native advertising audiences.

I don't have any assets, so I can't run a native advertising campaign

I don't believe you. I cannot think of a single business in existence – be it a solo painter and decorator, a local firm of accountants, a technology start-up or multinational brand – that does not have any assets that could be harnessed for native advertising success. If you are a butcher, baker or candlestick maker, tinker, tailor, soldier or spy, there is always an opportunity. If your business (or client, perhaps) has never created any content at all, doesn't even have a company website and is completely ignorant of social media, you can still run native advertising. How? Because businesses are built around people – they cannot exist without them – and wherever there are people there are stories. And as I've outlined already, the key asset you need for a successful native advertising campaign is a story. It will need tailoring and harnessing towards your brand, of course – and you'll undoubtedly need to sell it in to stakeholders – but it's all the assets you need.

Think like a native advertiser

Let us take the solo painter and decorator as an example. We will call him Ben. Ben has built his local business up over many a year; he knows a thing or two about running a small business, providing exceptional service, hiring and firing, and getting his taxes done on time. Ben prides himself on his professionalism and his personal relationships with his customers. Ben has seen and rectified many DIY disasters in his time; he's helped restore many local heritage sites, too. Ben knows what colour to paint a room that never gets any sunlight, and that Airbnb is a great tool to inspire those looking to spruce up their home interior. You've got all of this information from Ben – not via some long, convoluted 'editorial briefing document' or his blog posts – but from sharing a cup of tea with him for five minutes.

Look at the above. What do you see? If you see inane facts, you are not going to be a good native advertiser. I see content marketing opportunity. I see lots of stories. I see lots of story angles jumping out at me, that, should I need to – and should they fit into Ben's native advertising brief – I could turn into a native advertising campaign. We could, for example, run some native content across local media outlining local challenges small businesses face, as well as some tax return advice; we could run a post on Facebook along the lines of *10 Common Decorating Disasters and How to Fix Them*. We could, if Ben's budget and brief allowed, partner with a national publication like *Good Housekeeping*, or the *Evening Standard Property* website around the Airbnb tip ideas, too. One of their brand content journalists could interview Ben; we could expand the feature to a long-form video interview where Ben runs us through a selection of Airbnb interiors, highlighting to viewers how they can create these looks at home, too, and what colours they should choose to ensure they get it right. Lots of possibility – all from a story.

So don't let anyone tell you – and certainly don't think it yourself – that you don't have any assets to run a native advertising campaign. You do. You may need to work with an agency, platform or marketing professional to help draw these story assets out, but there's an entire industry of professional content strategists and content creators available to help. But before you recruit anyone, think. Spend a bit of time thinking about your objectives – think about how you can add value to your customers' lives – then sit down with your colleagues, your friends, or family and think about the story you want to tell.

Brainstorming: the power of a bad idea

There's a story from the very early days as a start-up that I and my business partner Francis Turner often share with our team. It is now many years ago, and it makes me cringe. But I think it's worth sharing to illustrate how no idea should be dismissed outright when brainstorming.

We were about four months into our entrepreneurial adventure together. And after a few months of courtship with a leading brand and potential client, we finally managed to get a foot in the door for a face-to-face meeting. This was a potentially big deal for us at the time; the brand was a leading retailer in the UK and household name – and to date all of our other clients had been either other start-ups or SMEs few people had heard of. Winning this client, we thought, would give us kudos in the market and open the door to lots of shiny new big name brand business – which, seeing as we were a completely boot-strapped business, we needed.

The day of the meeting arrived. We had our pitch down. Our presentation deck looked good. Francis, as lead on new business, led the presentation. He ran them through our deck and our proposition. Everyone looked impressed. Then the conversation turned to ideas. There was no brief to tender for the business we were pitching – the client knew they wanted 'content', but not much more. As the 'content guy' in the partnership, this was my turn to shine.

Conversation opened up – and I floated a few innocuous content ideas around, standard blog post ideas and tips, if I remember correctly. Then, as I am prone to do when brainstorming, it went a bit off track. I can't remember the exact question that led up to it – but one of the senior members of the client team asked me a direct question – something about what we would do for a new as-yet-unseen kitchen range. All eyes were on me. Expectation was in the air. I could feel Francis urging me to knock the ball out of the park and dazzle them.

The reply I blurted out was: '*sexy kitchens*'.

The response was muted. Floundering, I found myself freestyling on the theme for quite a while, expanding on what I actually meant with ever more odd content suggestions and distribution ideas: 'What your kitchen says about your sex life'; surveys around how many couples have had sex in their kitchen; celebrity kitchen secrets; infographics on how to 'sex up' your kitchen space; what colour tiles to choose if you are single, married or divorced! The list of bizarre ideas emanating from my mouth went on and on.

I left the meeting feeling as if I'd shot myself in the foot, and worse, Francis in the foot, too.

We laugh about it now, but afterwards I beat myself up for having such a bad idea: I felt like I had ruined a lot of Francis's hard work in getting us through the door and delivering a good presentation. I'd blown it for us.

We didn't hear from the brand for two weeks – which in the life of an early start-up feels like six+ months (but is almost an immediate response for a big brand!). When we did hear back we were surprised. They wanted to work with us.

We were ecstatic that we'd won their business – their feedback had been that they liked our different ideas, approach and creativity. We never ran with 'sexy kitchens', but we did subsequently work with this brand for the next three years and undoubtedly grew our business and their digital business as a result – on the back of a bad idea.

Since then I have had many, many bad ideas. I probably come up with nine or ten bad ideas a week. I enjoy sharing my ideas with the office – and encourage the office to share their ideas back. Good or bad. Sometimes we hit on a gem; sometimes we just laugh. It's good to laugh at yourself in digital media.

The point is that without any ideas – good or bad – we have nothing to differentiate ourselves from anyone else. If there's no glimmer of creativity, there's no reason to test anything. So don't dismiss any ideas as outlandish immediately.

So, what's your bad idea? It can't be as bad as sexy kitchens.

Do I need to do something different altogether?

Whether you have a lot of native assets that you think you could run, or whether you think you have no assets at all, a good question to ask yourself is: should I just run something completely different altogether? It's a good question to ask – and it shows that you are starting to think creatively about your native advertising options. What 'something different altogether' looks like, though, does need to be constrained. Whatever the 'different' is, it still needs to fit in with your overall brand voice, and 'different' in this instance really should be a means to meet your specific campaign KPIs.

The power of mobile

We've set out in this book to uncover everything you – as a marketer – need to know about native advertising. We've set out to show you how it is growing, too – and will inevitably become the dominant mode of digital advertising in existence. One of the main reasons behind this is how native advertising works with mobile. I've outlined this in earlier chapters, but it's worth reiterating here as it has to be a key influence on how you approach your native advertising campaigns. You need to remember that native advertising, more so than any other digital advertising format before it, is a mobile-first form of advertising.

What does that mean? It means that the majority of your audience will interact with your advertising, not via a laptop or desktop PC, but via a smartphone device. You can, of course, tailor your native advertising to just run against mobile, tablet or desktop, but in so doing you'll be alienating a portion of your customer base.

So it's important to generate a mobile-first viewpoint when thinking about your native campaigns.

How is content read on mobile devices?

We are still in the early days of fully understanding how we cognitively consume and digest the content that we read on mobile devices. Technology is advancing quickly, but so too is our familiarity with the concept of reading large amounts of content on our phones. Go back 15 years and most of us only read SMS messages and, possibly for a select few, e-mails, via our phones. Fast-forward to today and most of us consume large amounts of content – blog posts, news articles, emails, social media posts, comments, updates, chats, and even entire books – directly on our phones. How we actually process this information – and how it differs, for example, from reading content in print, or on a desktop, or even on a tablet device – is still something we need to study in more detail.

As well as screen size, the other element that can impact the capacity of a smartphone is the amount of time users can devote to a device. Phones, unlike our desktops and laptops, are used almost anywhere: which means that when you are using one to read something, you are at a far higher risk of being interrupted as you do so: you might reach your train stop; your partner may ask you a question; or, as is increasingly the case – your smartphone may interrupt you itself by letting you know you've received a new WhatsApp message, Facebook like, Twitter alert or e-mail. So the attention 'capacity' you give over when reading on a mobile device is very different from a desktop. Distractions are everywhere.

As a result, we could surmise that less is more on mobile, then. We can guess this from our own personal experiences as smartphone users, can't we? Shorter-form content that is easy to read is what hits the spot more often than not. But is this actually true? Is reading actually impaired by a mobile device? A 2010 study undertaken by the University of Alberta claimed it did. The study found that reading comprehension was impaired when content was presented on a mobile-size screen versus a larger computer screen.[2] Why, exactly?

The explanation given was rooted in our thought processes. It simply argued that as phone readers reading via a small screen saw less of the text at any one time, they had to rely more on memory to access the information they needed when reading. Or more simply put: readers on mobiles had to use their memories more when reading, because of the nature of the small screen.

But a similar study undertaken six years later and published in December 2016 showed different results. The study undertaken by the Nielsen Norman Group, of 276 participants, concluded that they found no practical differences in the comprehension scores of the participants, 'whether they were reading on a mobile device or a computer'. In fact, the study found comprehension on mobile was about 3 per cent higher than on a computer for content that was just over 400 words in length, and at an easier level to read. Why the difference in results? Could it be that over the last six years we've all become more accustomed to reading on smaller screens – and now the challenges the average person had reading on a small screen six years ago are no longer an issue? Possibly. But the answer is we don't actually know.[3]

The study did find that for longer content – just short of 1,000 words, written to a higher level – comprehension did dip on mobile, suggesting that it may well be that very difficult content is in fact harder to read on mobile than on a computer. More studies and more research on the topic needs to be undertaken to be sure, but it does raise some fascinating insights.

Assets

Tailoring your native advertising messages to fit different formats, then, is key. But it also means that your additional assets – your company website, your PDF downloads, your apps and social media properties – are all mobile-ready too. For example, if users click through to your site and are confronted with a 'find out more' form that you are hoping to use to generate sales leads, but it doesn't actually work properly for anyone accessing the page via the Apple IOS system, there's an awful lot of potential sales leads going missing there.

Creating your native advertising

Whether you are running a campaign via social media advertising, in-feed native distribution or content recommendation, the main assets of your advertising will normally consist of:

- a headline;
- a description (this will differ depending on publisher/platform used);
- an image thumbnail.

All placements will also carry some form of disclosure, clearly labelling the native content you are promoting as paid for. Increasingly this labelling is not controlled by the advertiser building the advertisement, but it's more often than not set in advance by the native platform and/or the publisher where the native ad unit will appear.

All platforms also allow for inputting the relevant website URL that you, as the advertiser, will want those who click on your ad to land.

The importance of headlines

Of the three main elements that will make up your native advertising preview, the headline is the most important. It is the one part of your native advertising that 100 per cent of your intended audience is going to see. Whether they click on your advertising or not, they will still read it – and it will offer brand recall and engagement as a result. If you want anyone to click on your advertising, the headline has to be just right.

Claire Austin, former Head of Audience (Social and Native Strategy), at King Content, Sydney, and now co-founder of Sprintlane, a business that enables other businesses to adopt a more agile way of innovating, believes that the headline is key to native advertising success:

> This is the hook so it needs to be good. In a digital world where there is millions of content being produced every day, if you want to be seen, you need to know your audience and know what will make them stop scrolling and click. It has

to be what I call 'thumbstopping'. Testing headlines is the best way to better understand what drives clicks, but remember they have to read the content too. High CTR does not mean engaged users; check your time on site, and subscriptions if you have them, for a true indication of success.

Writing effective headlines for your native advertising is part science and part art. It's about analysing and testing different combinations and styles; but it's also about trying something out for pure curiosity, experimentation and channelling creative messaging accordingly. It can be a challenge, even for seasoned content teams.

To help our internal editorial team working in our newly created content studio at ADYOULIKE, I drew up an internal document offering my thoughts and ideas on how to generate good native headlines. We call it the 'SLIP IT' test for native headline generation. In summary, all native headlines should make those who read them do one of the following:

- Smile
- Laugh
- Inform
- Provoke
- Involve
- Think

The SLIP IT test is a bit of a blunt instrument, but if you are new to generating headlines, use it as a starting point. Write 20 native advertising headlines for your brand and then measure what you create against the SLIP IT test. Remove any that fail to illicit one of these responses. They are boring. They will not work.

How to come up with native headlines

Look at magazine front covers

The purpose of a magazine front cover is to do much the same as what a native headline should do: attract readers and their interest. They are the original form of clickbait. We can learn a lot from magazine front covers.

Here are some example titles, taken from various magazines:

- EXCLUSIVE first pics of Beyonce's post-baby body
- The Inside Story of the Greatest Album Ever Made

- Get the Love You Deserve Now
- Get beach body beautiful with these shape-up tips
- Does he really love you?
- The Ibiza summer sounds you shouldn't miss
- 20 SENSATIONAL ways to promote your blog posts

Do these headlines pass the SLIP IT test? I think they do. Other proven tips for native advertising headline success:

- **Ask a question:** do not be afraid to pose the question that your target audience might be secretly asking themselves: 'Does he love me?' 'Do you need a new wardrobe?' 'Am I doing enough with my career?' This can grab people's attention and, of course, encourages them to click through to discover the answer.

- **The use of a pull quote:** a quote from the native content you are going to run can work really well, especially if it is part of an interview. For example, if you are looking to run a native campaign for a new movie, you could do something like this: 'Making the movie was my biggest challenge yet' – Hugh Jackman.

- **Challenge consumers:** 'Have you ever wondered what it would be like to own a mansion?'

What you are really looking to do with each headline is promote empathy with the reader; make them feel a part of the story your headline tells. Look at the above title examples – the majority all bring 'you' into the story. They help you build feelings of exclusivity; they impart information 'you' cannot afford to miss out on.

Additional tips

The tips below are popularly used by advertising copywriters, journalists and editors the world over. Some will work for your business, but all of them should help get your creative ideas flowing:

- **The opposite tool:** turn a negative into a positive. 'Good things come to those who wait,' or a Bupa ad: 'The patient will see you now, doctor' – highlighting the benefits of no waiting times. Add humour to something serious, or vice versa.

- **The list of three works well:** 'Friends, Romans, countrymen...', 'Hip, hip hooray', 'The Lion, the Witch and the Wardrobe'.

- **Contrasting pair:** 'live well, for less' or 'think globally, act locally'.

- **Alliteration:** always accurately awesome.
- **Puns:** use sparingly. These are generally frowned upon in advertising copywriting, but in newspaper terms are very popular – think tabloid newspaper headlines. So we can and should add a couple when relevant. Double-meaning puns are even better: 'This new product really sucks' – for example, for a vacuum cleaner. Use puns, but be careful not to be too cheesy! Try to turn them on their head.

For pun inspiration think about

- rhyming words, old sayings, popular sayings;
- song, film, TV or book titles that can relate to the product.

Dos

- Keep it simple – simple, conversational language.
- Do not be boring – duh!
- Feeling of exclusivity – talk directly to your reader – use 'you' and 'your' a lot.
- Use metaphors to create strong emotions.
- Evoke emotion – try to place your product or service in line with an emotion.
- Help your customers project themselves 'inside' the story – images, headlines, descriptions should all focus on this aim.

Don'ts

- Avoid negatives – even a passing negative is never well received by consumer or advertiser. If you can't be positive, don't be negative.
- Avoid overusing phrases such as 'best', 'top', 'amazing', or anything hyperbolic – unless you can back it up. For example if they have been voted best new car, say it. If not, do not call it best.

Images

The images that you use to accompany your native advertising are as important as your headline. Remember, the image thumbnail that accompanies your headline is going to be the most viewed part of your campaign. It's your opportunity to entice an interaction with your brand. It's your chance to showcase your content and your brand in the feed. Don't waste it. It's quite simple, I know, but it still surprises me how many advertisers don't think about imagery properly. From my own experience of running thousands of campaigns, image thumbnails showing human actions that evoke empathy perform best – three times better on average – as opposed to just running product images on the same campaign. So images are very very important. Show your product or service in use, up close, with an emotional connection obvious to see for best results.

What images you run with will depend on the content you are promoting, of course, but there are a few key rules to bear in mind for native advertising. We'll list these below.

Product images and logos: I'm sorry to have to tell you this, but no one wants to see a thumbnail of your new product in their feed. Unless it's something so amazingly unique – like a hover car, or a solid gold aeroplane – very few people are going to be enticed to pause in-feed by a product shot of your new washing machine or chocolate bar. And don't even go there with your company logo. Nothing could look less native than running your brand logo as the image thumbnail. Don't do it.

What should you do with images?

It's being proven time and time again that thumbnail images of people – preferably good-looking, happy people – work well in garnering attention. The personable approach is key, and the more you can capture the essence of authentic content, the better. So images of people using your product are OK, perhaps, provided they don't look too staged, or too much like stock image footage. For example, if you are an athletics brand, don't promote an image of your new product, run with an image of someone running wearing your product.

Here are some other things to think about with images:

- **Be careful with landscapes:** you may have the most amazing photograph of beautiful scenery to run with for your campaign – and the photo does look great – but what does it look like when it is condensed down into a thumbnail? On mobile? Is there anything in the foreground to draw attention to the image? If not, opt for something else.

- **Avoid clickbait images:** it's all too easy to get carried away with images when you start to think about what will attract user attention. Always try to find the right image to fit the content or product that you are promoting – but remember not to go overboard. Celebrity images, bikini shots, famous images, and humorous poses are well-known methods adopted with images for native advertising, but they only work in context if the content is relevant to the image. If not, what you are doing is obvious to see – and cheapens your brand persona. Sure, a bikini-clad pic may attract more clicks to your content, but for every user that clicked through to your content, there are possibly 99 more that have dismissed your brand as crass clickbait. No one wants that. Think about the value exchange.

Image rights and native advertising

When it comes to using images online it can feel as though there are 50 shades of grey. You do come across some strange practices. What you can and cannot do can seem confusing – and it can potentially be very costly for your business. You see a lot of images – of celebrities, for example – being used across social media and native ad campaigns. These are taken from the public domain in many instances. For example, images published to Twitter and other social media such as Reddit are often deemed in the public domain – though most are excluded from use for commercial activity, which can be confusing when you are creating content for commercial purposes.

Most others are taken from Creative Commons (Creative Comms) licences. A creative commons licence is one of several public copyright licences that enables the free distribution of an otherwise copyrighted work. You can find out more at Creativecommons.org. Wiki Comms is also a good search engine of Creative Comms image content. You can use certain images in certain ways, for certain types of content, provided attribution is given and full image credits listed on pages where the images run.

In my experience, when working with these sorts of assets it's often not 100 per cent clear if images are free to use for promotion or not. My advice, if you are in doubt, is to err on the side of caution and not use them. Either rely on your own business images (or images you take yourself), or alternatively sign up for an account with image library services such as Getty Images, istockphoto, or Shutterstock. For cheaper services – with lower-quality images but large databases that do the job if you are prepared to search a little deeper – check out clipart.com and pixabay.com (free).

CASE STUDY Social media native advertising: HappyFresh
and Instagram

HappyFresh is an online grocery platform designed and launched with the aim of getting people across Asia to shop for groceries using their mobile phones. It already has a presence in Malaysia, Indonesia, Thailand, Taiwan and the Philippines, and is expanding quickly.

Buying groceries online and on mobile is still a unique concept for Malaysia, as it is for most of Asia. So how do you encourage Malaysians to consider shopping in this way, while also attempting to drive app downloads?

The solution had to be on mobile and it had to be visually stimulating, ideally showcasing how easy it is to grocery shop via a mobile device. So they turned to Instagram advertising.

HappyFresh used video storytelling to encourage Malaysians to consider shopping for groceries on their mobile phone – and install the HappyFresh app. They created a video that visually walked viewers through the process, showcasing how easy it is to order fresh groceries via the app. The advertising was geo-targeted to reach the 3.6 million people in the Kuala Lumpur region who lived near HappyFresh stores that cater for mobile shopping. This meant that those who saw the advertising, would also be able to download and use the app. Through content and creative optimization that showcased different products and creative, depending on user behaviour, HappyFresh was also able to drive a 30% reduction in overall cost per acquisition.

Because mobile shopping is only available in selected stores, HappyFresh used geographic targeting to reach 3.6 million people who lived near participating HappyFresh stores in Kuala Lumpur an average of nine times each. This meant people who saw an ad were able to use the app, and not just engage with the brand's content.

HappyFresh optimized their ad placements across Facebook, Instagram and Audience Network so the right people were shown the right creative and products. This achieved a 30% lower cost per acquisition (CPA).

Results

- 3.6 million people reached;
- 30% lower CPA cost.[4]

Why it worked

Good content. Good targeting. Good use of data. This usually equals campaign success. This campaign works because HappyFresh were careful to ensure that the video ad served multiple functions. It showcased the app, yes, but it told a story too, which went a long way to allaying the fears many Malaysians had around using such an app: that the food delivered would not be fresh. Lastly, the video encouraged users to download and use the app – hence why it was such a good tool for driving down conversions. Creative optimization and geo-targeting to locations where the audience would be inclined to download and use the app ensured that there was no wasted ad spend.

View @happyfresh_my

Descriptions: supporting your headline

Not all native advertising units will run with a description – this often depends on the publisher or platform you are running with. But where they do, they need to be well crafted. Again, just like the images and headlines, the description – typically a 140–160 character content summary or introduction that runs below the headline – is going to be the most read part of your campaign. It's your opportunity to showcase what the content is about and entice a reader in.

Native advertising copy

The native advertising previews aside, when it comes to creating the longer copy that may run as part of your native content, remember that there are no established rules around how long or how short the content you create should be. You really do have a creative canvas to experiment with.

Do not be afraid to go into detail

Research from the 1950s – when advertorials in newspapers were common and were big business for advertisers and publishers – looking at reader habits around print advertorials found that the fall-off in readership from 500+ words was limited. If you still had a reader at 500 words, the chances are they were going to continue reading to 800+ words. Why? Because they are interested in the content. They are engaged. *Think about it*: how many long articles do you read online when you are really interested in a topic? Provided the content is presented well, written well and keeps you informed, there is nothing wrong with creating longer-form content.

In fact, the freedom that native content allows in this regard is undoubtedly one of its major benefits. No one wants to be confronted by a bland page of text. This didn't work in print and it certainly doesn't work online. So incorporate the following into your native posts:

- **Sub-headings:** sub-headings attract readers. At a glance it means they can decide whether to continue reading or click somewhere else.

- **Video:** embed a video within your ad copy. It is a sure-fire way to help the modern-day online consumer interact with your brand, and it keeps them engaged.

- **Quotes:** big, bold, punchy quotes can help break up the text and pull readers in. If possible, include external reviews of your product, or even customer testimonials; third-party testimony about how good your product or service is always works well for building appeal.

- **Images:** People like images. Add them to break up the flow of your content.

Video creative

If you are running video assets as part of your native advertising campaign, simply chopping up your TV ad, or pushing out some content marketing piece you created for your blog, is not likely to cut it. The way video content is consumed in-feed, on mobile, is completely different from other ways of viewing video online, or off. For success, you need to take into account a number of things. Follow these tips:

- **Dazzle with your opening sequence:** videos on Facebook and other in-feed distribution formats auto-play as users scroll through the feed. You only have a few seconds to 'hook' them in. So get to the meat of your video right off the bat.

- **Add captions and subtitles:** the majority of videos consumed on mobile devices, on platforms such as Facebook, are watched with the sound off. So if you fail to add subtitles and captions, you are missing a major opportunity to engage with your intended audience:

  - Think about the headlines you run to tease viewers into your video (see above tips).

- Think about your thumbnails, too – make it a great still from your video (see above image tips).
- Think about creating something shareable – videos are shared a lot on social media. Create a call to action, or shareable element in your video for additional reach.

Testing creative

Whatever you create for the above in terms of headline, thumbnails and descriptions, remember this: test them. How do you test them? You create more than one of each, for a start. If you are promoting the same webpage, experiment with three or four different headlines, descriptions and image thumbnails. After a few days of activity running across the same platforms, you'll likely be able to see what creative is working best. Do the same across every campaign you run. Make sure this is tracked and tagged correctly, too, of course.

If you want to say something, don't say nothing

Native advertising has developed as a way for brands to distribute and share content-led messages to a wider audience, at scale. But regardless of your distribution method, the best marketing messages that utilize a content approach are successful because of one thing: they have an idea behind them.

There is too much content being created and distributed online that has no idea behind it: all the gear, no idea. As Richard Cable, Bartle Bogle Hegarty's digital publishing director, put it in an article for *Campaign* in 2015:[5]

> where advertising is a marketing communication that interrupts what you are doing (whether you like it or not), content is a marketing communication that you choose to spend time with.

This is only true if your content has an idea behind it, or if the content you spend a lot of money on actually has purpose. Otherwise your content is, well, nothing. No one wants to 'spend time' with content that is like this – words on a page, an aimless video or random graphic. Shock horror – a shouty, aggressive ad that tells it like it is might be better than that!

'Buy this product' is a better message to push out than 'random piece with no real purpose'. It's content creation for content's sake. Don't do that. Have an idea. Create it. Share it. REPEAT. Simple, isn't it?

> The very best native advertising campaigns adopt a real-content approach – and are phenomenally successful as a result. So ask yourself: are you guilty of creating content without ideas?

Key creative points in summary

Struggling to get your head around native content? Follow a few of these tips to getting it right:

- **Tip 1: Think like a person.** You are writing content that you want your end user to engage with; you want them to like and share the content. So think like a person, not a brand. Yes, it is branded content, but that doesn't mean your target customer cannot enjoy the content you are promoting to them. It also doesn't mean that the content you write should read like an ad. It should read like an informative piece of content – that they like! You may want to follow these points: Write to entice. No one likes to be bored by what they read. The time span for online content to strike as a hit or a miss can be judged in split seconds these days. Make sure your opening paragraph is enticing: short, punchy, eye-catching sentences.

- **Tip 2: Use emotive words.** Words are important. Use simple sentences. Short sentences can get the point across. But use effective, emotive words that your customers respond to: 'terrific', 'best', 'first class', 'exclusive', 'breathtaking', 'top', 'excellent'. But be careful not to go over the top with over-sensationalism.

- **Tip 3: Reinforce the message** you are trying to get across in your headline in your opening paragraph. This will build trust and brand equity with your target audience.

- **Tip 4: Do not be afraid to go into detail.**

- **Tip 5: Don't assume readers are suckers!** Consumers are far savvier than we give them credit for. Don't write your content in a condescending way. Disclosure is everything with native advertising and brands should be happy to label their content as promoted by them. For content creators this means treating your target audience like real people.

- **Tip 6: Tell a story.** Speak to your target audience and their emotions. Don't be cynical, but engage with them on a personal level. It's hard with some brands, but every single product or service advertised fills a personal, emotional need for someone!

- **Tip 7: Take a risk.** Back up that risk. If you think something will work for a content piece for your target audience, try it, monitor it, analyse it, learn from it.
- **Tip 8: Don't be boring.**

CASE STUDY Social media native advertising: HSBC and LinkedIn

When global banking group HSBC was looking to interact with a key business audience via the promotion of its HSBC Global Connections content, they turned to LinkedIn. The challenge was to find an innovative way to engage with business audiences that are very short on time, but also very interested in real business insight. This challenge made LinkedIn's sponsored content a good fit.

HSBC harnessed geographic targeting of LinkedIn sponsored content to promote its new Trade Forecast Tool, and then utilized personalized statuses based on the data that was relevant to each particular market. HSBC were able to select and change content at particular times, on particular topics, depending on relevancy, and showcase this content in the LinkedIn feed. It was a strategy that worked, as the results below show.

Results

- 40,000 interactions with HSBC Global Connections content;
- boosted organic update impressions by 1500% and social interactions by 900%;
- created long-term value, attracting over 3,750 new followers to the HSBC Commercial Banking LinkedIn company page;
- delivered reach and engagement from over 50 industries;
- engaged with top titles including CEO, vice president, and director of operations.[6]

Why it worked

LinkedIn is a good fit for professional, business-related content, and HSBC maximized the opportunity that LinkedIn sponsored content allows. The results are impressive in terms of overall reach and in the relevancy and profile of those interacting with the content. Adopting a 'test and learn' approach of what content resonated best, at particular times, with an audience is also invaluable for any brand wishing to adopt a more customer-centric approach: all of the content consumption insights garnered from this campaign can be used again for future content and native strategies.

Get your creative juices flowing

Sometimes it's hard to be creative within your own business. Or rather it takes time to think 'outside' of the business, to think laterally about your overall marketing plans. The same is true if you manage a client day to day at an agency. The day-to-day minutiae of our businesses can and does take away our thinking time.

It's something I've struggled with myself at times; the reality of running an expanding digital start-up is that there are always immediate concerns to dedicate your time towards. So when you have to don your 'creativity cap' in the midst of it all, ideas are slow to come by. I'm not alone in this. In fact, if you speak to many people – inside and outside the 'creative industries' – few people actually believe they are at their most creative when at work.

My old university friend Daniel Glover-James is a copywriter at ad agency VCCP in London. He is holder of a coveted D&AD pencil and Kinsale Gold Shark, as well as the man credited with creating the 'Be More Dog' advertising concept for O2. Daniel believes the best ideas come when you are doing something else.

> I like to have a ponder whilst I'm running or cycling. I think it's called the alpha state. When your body is doing something, your mind becomes more free. More creative. I don't usually believe in that sort of nonsense, but in this case it does seem to work.[7]

So when it comes to trying to think objectively while at work, or when bogged down with thinking about work, we are often blocked. The ideas can't come because you are worried about execution – you know so-and-so from another department will block that idea, or fail to deliver the necessary assets; or you know the client will never go for a particular idea because you know they object out of principle to a particular type of marketing. That's when we freeze. Our ideas become stale. Complacency sets in and innovation says au revoir. That's not good for anyone. Ideas are all about taking risk, then quantifying their validity by backing them up to show how they will work.

So if you are reading this book, but failing to put what you are reading into context around your own business, the below is a creative exercise I've used in a number of workshops over the years. If you are a student of marketing looking to harness your creative native advertising skills, the exercise below is as close to a real-life content and native brief as you can get. It's completely made up – so any resemblance to any business you know (or celebrity for that matter) is purely coincidental.

An exercise in generating ideas for a native advertising brief

Read the brief below.

The background

Analysis of their own buying data and customer surveys by a leading florist has revealed a major change in consumer buying habits of flowers over the last six months: their big data analysis shows that more men are buying flowers for themselves, rather than just as a gift. A more detailed analysis has revealed that men are indeed buying flowers for themselves. In fact, the most popular flowers men are buying for themselves are yellow roses, inspired from the revelation in the press that leading Hollywood actors – and even rap stars – reportedly insist on having yellow roses with them at all times – as they are believed to be an ancient sign of virility.

Keen to capitalize on the growing trend and to challenge perceptions about men buying flowers for themselves, the florists have created their own 'Boys Bouquet' range of yellow roses. They want to promote this to young men in particular.

The client understands that success will not come overnight, but have allocated over $1 million for a six-month campaign. They are very open to exciting new ideas to promote this product.

A successful campaign will be judged on orders of the 'Boys Bouquet' from their online store.

The challenge

Changing the perception of buying flowers for themselves among men. Promoting the yellow rose as a masculine flower endorsed by celebrities – and the benefits of buying roses for men.

Target demographic: young men – 18–34 years old.

Assets available

A press release highlighting the data and the buying habits of men. The raw data is also available. The digital advertising campaign will coincide with a PR push, non-paid social media activity, and billboard advertising at major commuter hubs across key metropolitan areas.

So get started. What are you going to do with this brief? Where do you start? I'm not going to complete this brief for you, but to kick-start your thinking, here are a few questions to ask yourself:

1 Where does my target demographic congregate?

2 Are there particular devices that this demographic use more often than not?

3 What is the KPI of the campaign?

4 Are there 'soft' KPIs, such as perception, engagement, to consider?

5 Are there 'hard' KPIs, such as sales to generate?

6 Is it a new product or service to the market? If so, does the target audience need 'educating' about the benefits?

7 Will this campaign benefit from a particular type of native advertising product?

8 Is building topic momentum, social shares, and lots of social buzz the key metric for success?

9 Should the native advertising be humorous, or more 'educational' and how-to style, informative? Or both? Which will generate the most reach among my audience?

10 Is there enough budget to experiment with different products at first?

11 Is the client open to unique ideas?

12 Will the advertising campaign run in conjunction with other marketing efforts?
    If so, is there a way we can harness this activity/assets for native advertising efforts?

These are just some of the questions to ask yourself when you review a brief. I'm not going to tell you why you should ask yourself these questions.

Hopefully by reading this book, you know. I'm also not going to show you what I think the end proposal that you create for your 'customer' should look like. Otherwise you'll be encouraged to 'copy-paste' this proposal into your own creative thinking. Sorry, you are on your own!

That said, if you contact me via LinkedIn I'd be more than happy to read and rate your proposals. You can reach me on:

Twitter @DaleL_NativeAds

LinkedIn www.linkedin.com/in/dalelovell

Good luck.

Endnotes

1 MediaCom (19 October 2016) MediaCom unveils Feed Ready digital content service [online] www.mediacom.com/en/news/news/2016/mediacom-unveils-feed-ready-digital-content-service/ [accessed 28 March 2017]

2 Kate Meyer (11 December 2016) Reading Content on Mobile Devices [online] www.nngroup.com/articles/mobile-content/ [accessed 28 March 2017]

3 Budiu, R (13 April 2014) Scaling User Interfaces: An Information-Processing Approach to Multi-Device Design [online] www.nngroup.com/articles/scaling-user-interfaces/ [accessed 28 March 2017]

4 Instagram (2017) HappyFresh [online] https://business.instagram.com/success/happy-fresh/ [accessed 22 May 2017]

5 Cable, R (3 November 2015) Content without ideas isn't content: a retort to Dave Trott [online] www.campaignlive.co.uk/article/content-without-ideas-isnt-content-retort-dave-trott/1371060 [accessed 28 March 2017]

6 LinkedIn Marketing Solutions (2016) HSBC Case Study [online] https://business.linkedin.com/content/dam/me/business/en-us/marketing-solutions/case-studies/pdfs/05112016_LinkedIn_HSBC_CaseStudy_MM.pdf [accessed 28 March 2017]

7 Lovell, D (2014) The Creative Opportunity Around Native Advertising is Very Exciting [online] https://blog.adyoulike.com/tag/advertising-creative/ [accessed 28 March 2017]

Building a team for native advertising success

Within this section of the book I want to focus less on the native advertising product – and even its technical execution – and more on the mindset and personnel you need in order to succeed at native advertising. Without the right people in place who understand the nuances of native advertising and the fundamentals of what makes native advertising such a special marketing channel, you cannot hope to succeed.

It is the mindset required for digital marketing success. We'll look at what sort of individuals you need to hire – as finding these skills in one individual can be a real challenge. But we'll also look at how they will fit together as part of your wider native advertising team.

To succeed you'll almost certainly need to invest in a team that brings new skills to the table. But you should also recognize that you might need to adapt your own way of thinking to embrace some of these elements yourself, too. And you'll almost certainly need to try and convince those around you within your business that these skills are necessary to invest in – an area that, hopefully, this section of the book can help you with.

But before we get down to it, remember that all of this is worth the effort. Native advertising is going to dominate digital marketing in the years ahead. Whether it is the only digital ad format that 'wins out', as I've predicted, or not, it is certainly going to dominate. So if you want to invest your marketing budget in digital – and I can think of very few businesses that would not want to – then you need to adopt this mindset within your business – and fast.

Outsourcing expertise: get the most from an agency

The outsourcing of digital has always happened. The pace of change is so fast – and so constant – that learning new tools, technologies and ways of doing things is a full-time job. Brands, rightly, often feel as though they don't have the expertise to act quickly enough and not be left obsolete. Keeping pace with change is extremely challenging for those of us who ply our trade digitally, but it's also what makes it so exciting.

Outsourcing digital thinking is common. What do you do if you are a chief marketing officer (CMO) out of your depth digitally? You appoint someone else to run the digital element of the marketing function. This person is either someone that sits as the 'digital' expert internally, if budgets allow, or they are simply the digital agency appointed for the brand. Why do this? It's easier for a CMO to report to the board and executive team of a major brand that someone else in their team – or the agency appointed – is underperforming, rather than themselves. You'd rather replace an agency than replace yourself!

If you think you or your organization doesn't have the skills for digital, by all means outsource to a suitable agency, ad tech partner or hire in some expertise. But that's not the end of it. That should be just the start. The appointment doesn't mean you can outsource the thinking to your agency or platform partner: you need to understand what you are asking these partners to do for you, set some boundaries for success and work with them to ensure they have everything they need to do the best work possible for your business.

Many big name brands outsource the majority of their 'thinking' on all things digital to their agencies. Agencies are set up to be experts, whereas in-house brand marketers have to contend with a broader spectrum of brand-specific concerns that eat up a lot of their time and energy.

As Sir Martin Sorrell, founder and CEO of WPP, the world's largest marketing group, says, it is better for everyone if 'clients say "Let's try and work together, let's reduce the scope and improve the decision-making process on the client and agency side"… I find the best relationships are the first type, where we understand the pressures clients are under [because] we are under pressure ourselves.'[1]

Remember, agencies are not mind-readers. The best agency–client relationships are based on partnership; the more you know about what you want to achieve – and what can possibly be achieved through a marketing function – the better the work your agency can do and the better the results generated.

The changing shape of digital marketing

The old ways of thinking in marketing are no longer valid. Native advertising is part of this overhaul in marketing. Previous generations worked on marketing campaigns that were planned months in advance and looked to be executed efficiently by each corresponding member of a team. This meant that traditional marketing team structures almost always resulted in the creation of silos of knowledge, where information and ideas do not overlap. Teams and campaigns are run separately; for example, TV runs separately from print. These silos do not belong in native advertising.

Today's digital marketing increasingly takes the form of a more conversational always-on approach. It's a two-way street, where consumers talk back to brands. Brands therefore have to be more reactive to feedback and more immediate with their planning and execution. When marketing works like this, you increasingly need team members with a broad level of industry understanding and skills. Or to put it another way – your team needs to be agile. Native advertising is a fluid, malleable, anything-goes ad format; like the internet itself, it takes from hundreds of different influences and mixes them up to deliver something new and creative. The people who work in it need to act and think like this too.

You need the agility within your team to react. The winning combination for success in digital advertising is increasingly creativity, timeliness and platform – or, right idea, right time, right platform. Success is as much about getting your timing right as it is about the idea.

Interview with Melissa Wusaty, Content Strategist, Maxus

Describe your organization and your role

Maxus is a media agency made in the digital age. We were founded in 2008 and, from the outset, we recognized that in today's ever faster and complex landscape, clients want an agency that can help them navigate and lead change. We're unique. We embrace technology and innovation, challenging our clients to move forward, while remaining grounded by bringing them solutions that are simple, creative, effective, efficient and that will deliver a tangible benefit to their business – not just immediately, but over time. Our technology, effectiveness and data (TED) team sits at the heart of the agency and ensures that straightforward tech and data solutions are central to all the work we do.

We consider ourselves a global network of local agencies. With over 2,700 people in 70 offices across 55 markets, we have consistently been the fastest-growing media network in the world since our inception. We're proud to be part of both GroupM, the world's top global media investment management group, who have unrivalled scale in trading and technology to help us deliver client advantage, and WPP, the world's largest communications services group.

As a content strategist, my role is largely about interrogating briefs to provide clear strategic vision for content – asking hard questions, educating, forging cross-departmental processes, interpreting data and getting under the skin of a brand, the industry it's a part of and understanding its audience (future or existing) before any content is created. Essentially, I sit across the full breadth of content, from understanding and developing its role, the ideation and creation stage, to distribution and performance. My role sits in a specialist department called CHORUS – an award-winning collective of organic performance specialists, social and branded content practitioners, who work collaboratively to deliver purposeful content solutions. We're a global first for Maxus and what we do is unorthodox within a media agency, but this is also our strength as we have unparalleled understanding of audiences and their media behaviours.

How important is content in digital advertising?

To understand how important content is, you need to understand broader attitudes and behaviours. Advertising needs to move with people, not against. I very consciously chose 'people' over 'consumers' because this is the mindset we must adopt to get better at what we do – not only for the sake of helping our clients, but for the sake of anyone who goes online and gets overwhelmed, even anxious, about the amount of content available, which explains why anything that helps an individual filter what they spend their time on is growing.

Consumers, leads, accounts – this language is awful. The direction of advertising is firmly pointed towards personalization. Any brand that is able to curate their content towards the tastes of an individual while leaving enough room to discover something new will succeed. Content is pivotal to personalization, but it's not easy or cheap.

Content requires a complete shift in mindset and approach: if a piece of content doesn't do what's it's supposed to do, brands need to start getting comfortable with the fact that maybe what they're doing is just not good enough. At the end of the day, content should be designed for people and what they need – whether that's to be entertained or informed. The future of digital advertising won't favour the lazy but those who take a more considered approach, and this is why content (done well) has become so important.

Why do you think native advertising and branded content have become so successful?

When done well, it's more interesting than other formats. People are not fussed if the content is branded, just as long as it's high quality and fulfils a need. We need to remember that what people do online is completely in self-interest, and if your content – no matter how much media budget you have behind it or how well it's distributed – doesn't serve a purpose unique to that individual you're targeting, it will fall flat. This is why it's crucial to map content to an experience cycle, to ensure you're matching the right content to the right need at the right time on the right channel.

How do you measure success with your clients?

Like anything to do with content, measurement can't be a one-size-fits-all because different pieces of content serve different purposes, whether it's for awareness, consideration, conversion or loyalty. At Maxus, we measure different stages of the experience cycle and the content assigned to those different touch points. So rather than applying a campaign metric, we apply a stack model that better captures performance. We also measure over the short, medium and long term – this is where our TED team becomes crucial. What we measure and how we will measure success is also determined at the strategy and planning stage.

What makes a good content marketer? What skills do you need?

When we're thinking about what makes a good content marketer, we also need to think about what makes a good content culture within an organization. You could have the best talent, but if they're not supported by a wider culture and infrastructure conducive to collaboration, horizontality – whatever you want to call it – that allows them to bring together all the moving parts that makes best-in-class work, the role won't fulfil its potential. Agency to agency, brand to brand, what makes a good content marketer will vary because the same role will mean different things to different organizations. This isn't a bad thing, as diversity in remit, skill, background, experience, perspective fuels content and makes it competitive – but it's up to employers to thoroughly understand what they need when developing and hiring content roles, thinking about their culture, structure and overall readiness.

Outside of this, the best content marketers possess a mixture of hard and soft skills – and I would stress it's the soft skills that distinguish the best. Foundationally, they understand the nitty-gritty of performance, how to interpret data to make sure decisions are informed by insights, not just creativity. They have a firm grasp of how content performs on-page via organic performance and off-page via owned and paid media. They should be organized and consistent in their approach, knowing when to loop in other teams.

They think inside out – meaning they truly understand the brand, its vision, the role for content in that vision across the entire experience cycle, but also the wider world outside of that brand and how certain things will impact content. They place the needs of their audience at the core of what they do, which ultimately makes their work purposeful, accountable and measurable.

What truly makes an outstanding content marketer is when we start thinking about the areas that can't be boiled down to a science. The intelligence-gathering and interpretation side of content is absolutely essential, but content will always need a certain type of creativity. Strong abstract thinking. An editorial eye. Conviction in hunches. Obsessed with detail. How messages can be conveyed across all forms of communication – whether it's seen, read or heard. An emotional sensitivity. The ability to foster creativity in their team. The best content marketers don't have time for church and state arguments – they unify and break down silos.

Do you think there's a need for future training/skills in this area?

Agencies and brands alike need to become innately customer experience focused. I cannot stress this enough. Competition in price and product, for the most part, has completely eroded away, and what will sway a potential client or customer will be how efficiently touch points serve their purpose. That can be anything, whether it's an app, website or beyond. Content will be at the heart of this shift to personalization and we will need a whole new array of skill sets to do this right. I don't foresee it becoming a matter of content marketers becoming experts themselves, but getting themselves to a stage where they're familiar and comfortable working with entirely new areas – UX (user experience), CRO (conversion rate optimization), behavioural economics, psychology and perhaps even linguistics with the rise of voice search.

What do you think the next 10 years holds for native advertising?

Over the next few years, I hope we will see advertising embrace a more holistic understanding of content beyond production – we need to take responsibility for the rise of ad blocking and triggering a wave of negative sentiment towards advertising. The biggest risk for an organization investing in content is their target audience not caring. Do something purposeful. Give people a reason to care. Otherwise, don't bother. Content is too expensive and requires too much to do it wrong.

Content fails when its success is the responsibility of few. Putting the right team in place, supporting them with the right content culture and infrastructure, to produce less but better will be the way forward. This goes hand in hand with measurement and ROI. Thinking about what needs to be tracked and measured prior to production is the smartest thing a content marketer can do, but most of all, understanding that one metric, measured over a short period, is not going to accurately capture true performance or the long-term benefit of content. We need to start getting into the habit of measuring content over the short, medium and long term.

T-shaped marketers

If you have read up on marketing theory at all, you may have come across the phrase T-shaped personalities. The term has been popular at certain times in digital circles to describe the best types of people to have in place for particular roles.

The concept of T-shaped personalities essentially explains how marketers need to have broad experience and skills across marketing, but that they also need to cultivate a real specialism in one particular area. For example, a digital marketing manager may have worked across multiple parts of digital marketing – search, social media, content, pay per click (PPC), programmatic and display advertising – giving them a broad horizontal understanding of much of the modern digital marketing world, but they may only really have a deep 'expert' level understanding of one of these disciplines – social media, for example.

The benefits of T-shaped personalities are that they have advanced problem-solving capabilities within one particular field – gained from their deep-level expertise in one particular specialism, but also good communication skills and a breadth of understanding in wider issues. For industries where learning never ends and new technologies and new categories of expertise are emerging, the ability to combine expert know-how in one field, while maintaining the ability to communicate to a wider team effectively, is paramount to success.

π-shaped marketers

Econsultancy CEO Ashley Friedlein wrote a very interesting piece for *Marketing Week* on this topic in November 2012.[2] In the piece Friedlein argued that the T-shaped profile of marketers was outdated and that marketers needed to be pi-shaped – π – essentially those with skills in 'left brain' (maths, data, analytics) and 'right brain' (creative) disciplines. He claimed that marketers today need to be both 'analytical and data-driven, yet understand brands, storytelling and experiential marketing'. I couldn't agree more with this analogy. You need 'two brains' to be a modern digital marketer, for sure: you have to be analytical and creative. You need to be creative enough to develop great ideas and be able to understand and commission content, but you also need to be able to carry out analysis on what works, dive into the stats and use technology to analyse results. You need to understand that everything you do in digital – once content is involved – is part art and part science.

It's something that has been brought to the fore even more so in recent years by two big developments in digital: big data and content marketing.

Big data

Data is everywhere in digital. There's so much that we don't know what to do with it. It is a dream for analytic left-brain obsessives who love to live and breathe data.

Content marketing

Content marketing, the process of creating interesting content for your intended audience, as most marketers can testify, has been known to awaken the inner Hemingway and Dali in right-brain-leaning marketers. In the content marketing sphere there is increasingly the need to develop pi-shaped ways of thinking in order to meet the demands of content-led initiatives.

If your digital marketing is in the hands of an individual that is only left brain or right brain, or there is no joined-up thinking, the results, to put it bluntly, can be a complete mess.

Left-brainers can become crippled with data overload; they battle with often conflicting results that leave them unable to commit to anything, second-guessing their decisions.

Right-brainers operating on their own devices can spend all their time and budgets commissioning ideas that do nothing but boost their creative vanity and add nothing to their brand. It's creativity with no commercial purpose behind it. At either extreme, both give many a marketer a bad name (especially among disgruntled financial directors).

Systematic and narrative thinkers

Nick Law, Global Chief Creative Officer for advertising agency R/GA, in an interview with the IAB in September 2014, explained how his teams are often made up of systematic thinkers and narrative thinkers, which in today's story-led, data-driven world is so important:

> When you have a systematic thinker and a narrative thinker, you get this lovely tension between simplicity and possibility.[3]

The pitchfork team structure

> Really creative people are fascinated by 'new' stuff. But that doesn't just mean new technology. It means stuff that is new to them.[4] (Dave Trott, Creative Mischief)

As digital marketing becomes ever more based on technology, data and content creativity, in order to be successful, businesses will no longer be able to get away with simply hiring one or two pi-shaped marketers for their teams. That leaves too much room for error in critical areas where real expertise is required and already means the difference between success and failure in digital marketing for a brand.

For success, brands really need to develop a psi-shaped, or pitchfork-shaped, skillset within their teams. And if you are building a native advertising capability for your business, this is the strategy and the team model you need to adopt.

Psi – the Greek letter Ψ, which looks like a pitchfork – is the symbol that will symbolize modern marketing teams the most. Whereas T and pi marketers have a broad knowledge base running across the top of their marketing know-how and one or two distinct specialisms, or capabilities – right-brain and left-brain thinking capabilities – the pitchfork-shaped marketing department model is different.

The individuals involved are different. The individuals involved do not have to be T- or pi-shaped generalists; they can be specialists in distinct areas. They can be I-shaped personalities. They have no broad knowledge at all, but they may be experts in one particular niche.

They may have spent time as specialists in particular sectors of marketing; search, content, social, for example; or, something which is increasingly seen as beneficial, they may have specialized in particular fields from outside of marketing altogether: journalism, copywriting, filmmaking, data analysis, or computer science, for example. During this time they may have developed particular traits or ways of thinking that are mostly left brain, or right brain, centric. Some, if not all, will make no apology about being more one way than the other.

What businesses do with this expertise is crucial. They need to bring together the myriad individual areas of expertise they require, put them all in the same team and task them with the end goal of creating relevant, accountable content-led marketing. The crucial thing is that they have expertise. With direction, they know how to harness this knowledge towards an additional, communal end goal: the goal of creating powerful native advertising.

Relying on individuals to do all of this work – when even the smallest digital marketing campaign creates reams and reams of data to wade through – is just no longer realistic. This is where the pitchfork model comes in. So what does the ideal digital marketing team look like in more detail?

1 Creative

The right prong of your pitchfork should cover creative. This is the narrative side of your marketing channel. The individuals in this team should always be tasked with the challenge of 'How do we share this information in a story?' They may look at life in a different way from others, and see the connections that others do not. They should come at tasks with a hunger to condense messages into engagement. 'What's in it for our audience?' should always be on their lips. They should think like publishers and intuitively know what that audience is looking for. Of course, they should also know how to construct, commission and curate the content that you look to create as a brand, too.

Potential hires outside of marketing: journalists, editors, videographers, bloggers, PR, copywriters, designers, academics, artists.

2 Data

The left prong on your marketing department pitchfork should be dedicated to data. This is where your big data analysis comes in. This is where you really need to tap into some expertise to future-proof your digital marketing. This area of your marketing channel should be tasked with pouring over all the data your business has access to: whether it's customer insight, marketing performance reports, or external data relevant to your business or industry; these are the data-miners tasked with finding the data gems for

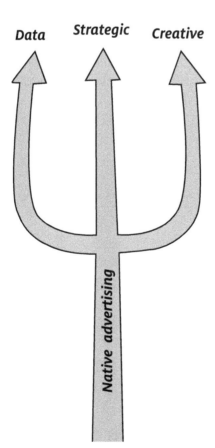

your digital marketing success. Without this important analysis, you are walking in the dark.

Potential hires outside of marketing: data analysts, engineers, accountants, scientists, statisticians, IT, web development, finance professionals, bankers.

3 *Strategic*

The central prong of your marketing team pitchfork is equally as important as the other two, if not more so, and is dedicated to strategy. This is the core that holds your native advertising and digital marketing function together. It is likely going to be where your overall team management lies. The individuals in this team are more likely to be T- or pi-shaped personalities than I-shaped, as they will need to have a broader understanding of wider business objectives to formulate strategy. Their key role will be the ability to take content, data, business objectives, budgets and briefs together and formulate a winning digital strategy. It's not an easy role, which is why it's increasingly necessary to ensure these individuals are well informed – and well supported – with the relevant left- and right-brain expertise that modern digital marketing requires.

Potential hires outside of marketing: managers, business leaders, entrepreneurs.

The model for native advertising success

Over the years I've worked with different clients that have been stronger on one aspect of content and native over another. Some have had fabulously exciting creative ideas, but were often divorced from reality when tasked with executing such ambitious plans on tight budgets. Others had very few creative ideas, and didn't seem to want to execute any ideas without data to back it up, which leads to a conundrum: you need to at least test and execute on some marketing in order to get any data to analyse in the first place. Others – and these are the easiest to work with – have had excellent strategic objectives and understood what they wanted to achieve, but needed support in execution. The ones I've enjoyed working with combine all three. This is when content-led digital advertising works.

If you look at the most successful teams in digital today – within agencies and corporations – and scratch beneath the surface, you'll see a version of the pitchfork-shaped model. Time and again it will be the brands that combine these three mindsets and abilities, pushing the boundaries in the process, that will be rewarded with digital marketing success.

Cultivate the right marketing mentality

Developing a pitchfork-shaped marketing function does have its challenges. Integrating different personalities, fostering cooperation between different ways – and speeds – of working, and championing a shared goal all have their challenges. It's impossible without the right management in place and full business buy-in. Hiring the right people who have expertise in a particular discipline, but want to use it in a marketing field, can be hard too.

So if you can't hire it, how do you cultivate it? Here are a few tips:

Encourage the development of expertise

If you currently have a team that covers all aspects of brand content and native advertising together, think about breaking this down into specialisms. You may already be able to see who in your team has an eye for data analysis, or content ideas. Encourage them to work more closely on specific aspects of the native advertising process that they are good at – and preferably enjoy. To avoid silos developing, ensure that all areas share their expertise regularly – so that the entire team can see how this has impacted and improved on your overall business marketing. Encourage strategists to spend time working within the creative and data prongs, too, in order to widen their knowledge and share expertise.

Hire from outside the industry

Creativity comes from new ways of thinking – and introducing new team members with specific skillsets from outside the industry is a great way to increase creativity for your entire team. Bring an ex-journalist, engineer or even a teacher into the team for a whole new strand of expertise and thinking.

Highlight success: create company-wide buy-in

It's easy to think that all of your creative ideas will come from your creative team, but that's not the case. You'll be surprised how often – when given the opportunity – a wider team can offer up some inspirational ideas. So share your native advertising goals with your wider business team: every single employee will be familiar with your product – and more often than not the digital channels you are promoting your content on – so highlight what you've done already and how it performed with the wider business for input. You might be surprised what comes back.

Embrace the pitchfork

In summary, the future of digital advertising is increasingly going to be defined by content. Brands will need to develop ever more interesting content ideas to cut through to their target audience. Marketers will need to make the business case for content; data will be key in making the case and calculating return on investment. To do all of this well, businesses need to embrace the pitchfork.

Endnotes

1 Chahal, M (4 February 2016) Sir Martin Sorrell on digital, cost-cutting and client-agency relationships [online] www.marketingweek.com/2016/02/04/ sir-martin-sorrell-on-digital-cost-cutting-and-client-agency-relationships/ [accessed 28 March 2017]

2 Friedlein, A (7 November 2012) Why modern marketers need to be pi-people [online] www.marketingweek.com/2012/11/07/why-modern-marketers-need-to-be-pi-people/ [accessed 28 March 2017]

3 Minnium, P (2014) Balancing Storytelling and Systematic Thinking: A New Model for Digital Creative Brilliance [online] www.iab.com/news/storytelling/ [accessed 28 March 2017]

4 Trott, D (2009) *Creative Mischief*, Loaf Marketing, London

The seven habits 11
of highly effective
native advertisers

In this chapter I want to focus on you – and the habits that you need to culti-vate in order to be an effective practitioner and champion of all things native advertising. There are some key personal attributes and areas of expertise native advertisers should look to cultivate. Whether you are a marketing student reading this book as you've heard about native advertising, a senior executive looking to introduce native advertising at a publishing business, or a brand marketer keen to experiment with native advertising, the below points are worth noting, sharing and championing.

So, what makes a successful native advertiser?

1 They have a start-up attitude

Whether you work for a large organization, are a student, or a solo business owner, the very best native advertisers have a start-up mentality. What do we mean by this? They are pioneers. They are energetic and open to new ideas and possibilities. They have imagination. They can see opportunity where others see only obstacles. They are happy to embrace change, have eagerness to experiment, and, crucially, always look to learn. For them, a closed door is something they need to kick open, not move away from.

2 They understand the feed

I've continually referenced throughout this book what I term the 'collec-tive campfire' of modern digital life. This is the feed. Our lives increasingly rotate around the feed. We look for stories on the feed; we share our own stories on the feed; our likes, dislikes, interests and tastes are cultivated on the feed. Without the feed, our lives are incomparably dull. Any effective native advertiser needs to instinctively be aware of this. The success or failure of your native advertising will depend on how it works in-feed. Native advertisers that get the feed understand the importance of headlines – this is the one part of your advertising message that 100 per cent of your target audience will see, whether they click on it or not. Headlines are the currency for success.

3 They get content

We've talked about content a lot. The power and psychology of stories is a fundamental part of human life and development. To be an effective native advertiser, you need to be aware of the value of content. You need to think like a publisher; think like your audience – and then tailor your advertising messages towards them with relevant, interesting content. Without it, you can't expect to fully reap the benefits of native advertising.

4 They get advertising

This is something that often gets overlooked when talking about native advertising, particularly by publishers who sometimes place too much emphasis on content, tone of voice and thinking like a publisher. Yes, I know I've encouraged exactly that in the above, but it's also important not to go too far the other way. Remember the point of what you are doing all of this is for: it's to build your brand and, ultimately, to sell more. It's not to create some cool branded content that will win a publisher an award. A lot is written about engagement in modern advertising. Thanks to digital and changing consumer relationships with advertising, success today is all about quietly offering an opportunity to engage with your target customer via good content at numerous touch points. This is true. But how do you engage someone you don't know without disturbing them first? From my experience, your customers do not mind being interrupted by a native advertisement if it is done in an informative or humorous way. So remember the advertising element in native advertising.

5 They know what success looks like

Each type of native advertising has its rightful, effective place in the marketing mix. It's such a broad term that saying you run native advertising is almost equivalent to saying you run 'ads online'. To be an effective native advertiser you need to be able to understand the difference between the different native advertising products that are in existence – and choose which ones are right for you.

Different native advertising formats work in different ways. Different strategies deliver different results. The best native advertisers know what success looks like. They know what they want to – and can – achieve at the start of a campaign, not at the end of it. They create native strategies with this in mind and execute towards these goals. This is what you should do too.

6 They get technology and data

Native advertising technology sits at the cutting edge of digital advertising. Whether it's using data and targeting to effectively deliver ever-more nuanced content-led advertising messages, simplification of the buying model and the introduction of real-time optimizations via programmatic, or the adoption of ground-breaking artificial intelligence, native advertising is built on technological innovation. And the very best native advertisers and native campaigns fully utilize this technology to generate results. They embrace new technology, not run away from it.

7 They know it's a team effort

The best native advertisers always recognize that they cannot do everything themselves. Whether they are left-brain or right-brain leaning, or well-rounded T-shaped personalities, or not, it doesn't matter; to get the best from your native advertising, it's always better to work as part of a team. The best advertisers are always part of a team. But even if you are the only person responsible for native advertising within your organization – and the only one tasked with setting up, running and measuring the effectiveness of a campaign – you do not have to work alone. You can still ask your colleagues in other departments for input on content ideas; or look online to relevant forums and groups for support.

Alternatively, some of the most successful native advertisers I know admit to knowing next to nothing about the mechanics of running a native advertising campaign. They were smart enough to recognize their own limitations – both individually and within their business – and recruited some external assistance to plan and run their native advertising campaigns for them. They were clever enough to recognize the content marketing and native advertising opportunity for their business, but they were super-smart to outsource the execution to experts.

Interview with Hannah Meium, Director of Branded Content, Mashable

Mashable is a media and entertainment company for superfans. We're not for the casually curious. Our proprietary Velocity technology suite gives us the unique ability to combine creativity with data. Our entertainment series and editorial coverage are smart, clever, ambitious, in-depth and first. We devour culture and tech. Our ideas shape the future and we speak to new influencers – the early adopters who obsess with us around the globe.

As Director of Branded Content, in my role I oversee all of our work that we create with our brand partners.

What types of brands run native ad campaigns with you?

We partner with a variety of brands on our branded content. Anywhere from tech to finance to auto to entertainment. My background is on the brand side; I'm a big fan of brands and I truly believe that brands have great stories to tell that can entertain, inspire and inform audiences. We love partnering with brands and helping them find those great stories. Great content doesn't need to shoe-horn a product message in; it can provide value to a reader and still deliver on a client's KPIs.

Why do you think native advertising has taken off and become so successful?

I think native advertising has taken off because of how cluttered the advertising and media space has become in the last few years. Brands are constantly on the lookout for new and authentic ways to reach their audiences. Partnering with publishers is a great opportunity for exactly that – authentic storytelling and targeting a known audience. By partnering with publishers, like Mashable, brands can leverage a publisher's voice and their established audience to share their brand messaging. Trust is critical for success.

PART FOUR
Native advertising in a wider business context

The business of digital 12

Native advertising sits in the cross-hairs of major digital trends. The rise of mobile, content marketing, programmatic buying and selling of advertising and digital publisher revenue all influence and are influenced by native advertising. As such, in order to fully appreciate the rise of native advertising, it's important to take a look at the wider way in which digital is disrupting the traditional media landscape. If you understand a bit about how money is made in digital – and by whom and when – hopefully you will be able to understand where native advertising has come from, and why it is so important to the future of digital advertising as a whole.

This chapter is a brief introduction and commentary on some key business digital trends and characteristics that influence and impact native advertising.

The advertiser, agency, ad tech, publisher matrix

It is a truly complex network of relationships that underpins today's digital media. There are labyrinthine connections between a host of different vested interests, which are not always apparent on the surface. These relationships go far beyond native advertising, of course, and underpin global multi-billion-dollar-a-year industries. But it is important to understand something of this in order to know where native advertising fits in, how it is disrupting existing relationships and why certain relationships are the key drivers of innovation in the space.

The age-old media model was either

Advertiser → Agency → Publisher (Media owner)

or

Advertiser → Publisher (Media owner)

The advertiser briefed the agency on things such as creative direction, budget, core objectives, available assets. The agency took this brief and went to their media owners to see what ideas they could come up with. If successful, a media agency would book the campaign spend with the media owner and manage, on behalf of their client, the media buy, reporting back on the success or failure of that campaign. This was how non-digital advertising worked, by and large, for generations. It worked very well.

But the above model causes some issues in digital. Unlike print media – where the work of the agency is largely complete once the creative asset is delivered to the publisher – digital ad campaigns are living, breathing entities that need constant nurturing for optimal performance. The campaign launch date in digital is the 'go' for lots of spinning plates to start: agencies have to watch everything – monitor performance, improve performance, update the client and deal with their ongoing demands, all at the same time. This is very hard to do across hundreds of publishers and multiple campaigns. From a digital campaign perspective, it means that a media agency has to speak to lots of media owners – big and small – and manage all of their creative, tags, tracking, reporting, measurement and performance one by one.

Ad tech helps

This is where technology has helped. Advertising technology, or ad tech, has developed as a way to assist in scale. Ad tech network businesses promise to assist in agency campaign delivery by offering a single point of entry to work with across multiple publishers, plus technology to help with set-up, reporting, optimizations, performance, measurability and reach.

So the modern model for large-scale advertising can look like this:

Advertiser → Agency → Ad tech → Publisher → Customer

But in reality there's a whole lot more. Now we have programmatic trade desks. These trade desks are set up (often by agencies) to manage ad spend for advertisers via sophisticated automated software and real-time marketplaces. Trade desks promise expertise, economies of scale and better ROI than running direct. They also work with ad tech and publishers. So the relationship can look like this:

Advertiser → Agency → Trade desk → Ad tech → Publisher → Customer

The above is a super-simplified look at the landscape. What it actually looks like is more like the flowchart on page 167 – and even that is a very simplified version.

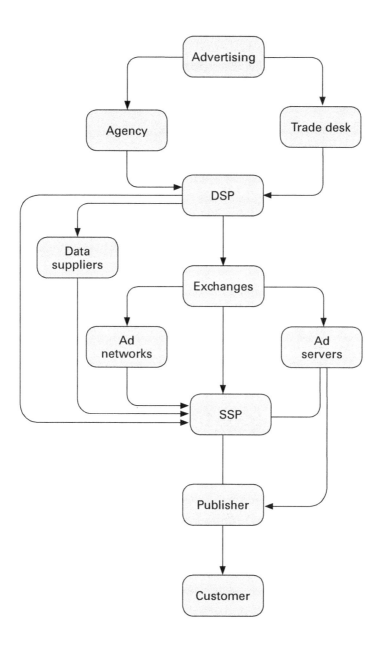

For a more details look at Luma Partners Lumascapes: www.lumapartners.com/resource-center/lumascapes-2.

You have technology services, you have demand-side platforms (DSPs) and sell-side platforms (SSPs), you have exchanges and ad networks; you have data suppliers and retargeting businesses, ad servers, tracking providers, third-party reporting tools, creative optimizers and much more besides, all in the mix. It's a labyrinth. The ad tech value chain from advertiser to publisher is certainly overly complex. What you need to remember is that everyone throughout the chain takes a cut, either directly from the advertising money as it is spent, or on set technology charge fees. Everyone is looking for growth, for margin and to win at scale. It's a complicated network of relationships buying and selling to one another. What are they actually trading? More often than not it's impressions: eyeballs and views.

Native advertising can sit with, and often be bought by, many along the chain. An advertiser could book directly with a publisher, or with a native ad tech business; a trade desk could book directly with both, too, as could an agency, or a DSP (demand-side platform). There's no issue with this. It's the sign of a super-fluid market with fewer barriers to trading than ever before – but it is confusing.

It's important to understand the market forces driving technology within the digital advertising eco-system: it strikes at the heart of how people actually make money with online advertising. It is these commercial forces that have helped lay the foundations for native advertising success, but that continue to cause challenges too.

How is digital advertising bought?

When an advertiser buys a print ad – let's say, for example, a full-page magazine spread – it's quite obvious to most people what they are buying. It's a physical property, printed thousands of times in a magazine – on a specific page, for a specific issue, which is then distributed to a certain number of people (who either pay for the magazine, or pick it up for free). How much the advertiser pays for this ad will depend on how many copies of the magazine are regularly printed and/or sold. This determines the reach of that publication, for which savvy ad sales executives know how to charge at specific rates. As the sale is made and the ad is built, most people involved understand that they are working towards having a finished ad, ready for print.

But what do you buy when you buy something digitally? Digital advertising is different. In the vast majority of cases (some small publishers aside), what you buy is an action – either a view of your advertisement, or a click on your advertising messages. Transactions are not, pay $XX and you can expect to be on this site or group of sites for a specific amount of time.

Digital media is bought and sold on an impression (view of your ad), or action (click, or video view). Native advertising is no different – although some branded content publisher partnerships will come with some sort of fixed tenancy basis, too. You buy audience – or eyeballs – with digital ads, not specific ad space for a fixed amount of time.

If this doesn't make sense, let's look at a brief, hypothetical example.

I am a famous washing detergent brand. I want to advertise on digital. So I take out an ad. As an advertiser you pay for 1 million ad impressions to run on a specific website, or group of websites, at a specific rate. Let's say I buy 1 million ad impressions for $5 per thousand views ($5 CPM). I will basically be charged $5,000 for 1 million views of my ad over the course of a month. But what if the website I advertise on has 30 million views per month? The publisher can, potentially, sell another 1 million impressions at the same time, for the same amount, if they have the capability to serve 1 million more ads, which they do. The publisher could actually sell 29 million more impressions on their site at the same time. So, the publisher could feasibly sell 30 × 1 million ad impressions at $5 CPM. That would equal 30 × $5,000 = $150,000. It's like selling that print magazine ad 30 times over. That's good business if the publisher can sell the space. All the publisher needs are more visitors to their site and some willing advertisers.

The crucial thing to remember here is that the economics of modern digital media is driven by volume: more visitor numbers equals more revenue. Advertisers buy on impressions; they want more eyeballs. Media properties looking to make more money must then, by default, find more website visitors.

Publisher arbitrage

So publishers need visits: eyeballs to their website means cash in the bank. Why? Because in the digital publishing economy, a set of eyeballs equals money. Each impression can be worked back to an earning equation. The more eyeballs, the more money you can potentially make. It's that simple. The same is true offline, of course; newspapers and magazines are driven by the continual need to boost circulation figures.

But when all you are looking for is a visit to your website – rather than the need for someone to actively seek out and pay money to physically buy your publication – or to drive a subscription paywall model sign-up, it is considerably easier to do this in digital.

How publisher arbitrage works

Digital publishers – after they've populated their sites with advertising units and tallied up the rates they'll receive per view – know how much money each visit to a page will net them. Let's, for argument's sake, say it's $0.10 per view, per page. That now gives the publisher a cost to work against in terms of driving website visitors to their site. If they can get a visitor to their site for, say $0.05, they will make 50 per cent profit per view. Once they know this, they can scale up accordingly. I can't think of many businesses that wouldn't be happy to spend $500 to receive $1,000 back.

Now the holy grail for publishers is to receive natural, returning visitors: people that seek out your publication as a content hub. This means you make 100 per cent in ad revenue from these users, as you've not paid to drive them to your site. But to get to this level takes time – and great content, which is usually expensive to produce, so it's easier, quicker and more affordable to just buy in visitors.

Savvy publishers looking to boost their website visitors increasingly use content as a 'hook' to draw visitors in. They create eye-catching headlines – as they have always done in the pre-digital age. But they also increasingly use paid-content distribution methods, too – social media advertising and content recommendation mainly – to amplify and extend the reach of this content.

These are tools that are very much a part of the modern digital publisher's arbitrage toolkit.

CASE STUDY   Content recommendation: The Singapore Economic Development Board and Outbrain

The Singapore Economic Development Board (EDB) is the government agency in charge of attracting foreign direct investment to Singapore. In March 2014, the EDB relaunched Singapore Business News (SBN), a digital publication covering key Singapore foreign direct investment announcements and Asian business trends.

The Singapore EDB wanted to grow SBN's subscriber base and share their content to the larger US business audience. The EDB, via their media agency MEC, partnered with Outbrain in April 2014.

The EDB were able to tap into Outbrain's 190 million unique visitors in the US to connect with new audiences and drive traffic to the SBN website from top publishers. With a reach of over 190 million unique visitors in the US alone, Outbrain helped the EDB connect with new audiences and drive traffic from premium publishers.

Results

- 40% increase in daily traffic to SBR within 6 months;
- 900 new visitors daily;
- 400% increase in headline click-through rates;
- 3-minute average website dwell time;
- 66% increase in engaged users since campaign launch.[1]

Why it worked

This a good example of using content recommendation to boost content engagement with relevant audiences in a specific market, at scale. The campaign worked because the quality of the content promoted by SBN was very high, but also because the publisher environment promoting the content was relevant too. The campaign was further boosted by ongoing content optimization to extensively improve the headline click-through rate and the publication of regular, fresh content. This is evident from the average three-minute website engagement time and the two-thirds increase in engaged users since campaign launch.

Gallery views: publisher arbitrage in practice

Ever noticed that sometimes when you click on an eye-catching headline online, you are often taken through to a website where the pages are literally covered in other content ads? This is publisher arbitrage in practice. Frequently when clicking through to content, you are taken through to a gallery page – and encouraged to click through page after page of the gallery. Ever wondered why? It's not for any aesthetic reason – these pages are relatively annoying in terms of user experience. It's all to do with page views. Every page you click on equals more ads you've seen – more impressions – and more ad revenue for the publisher. It may just be a few cents per visit, but multiply that by the thousands, or millions, and suddenly you are making big money. Galleries are a boon to monthly page view statistics, which publishers use to highlight growth, audience size and potential advertising revenue.

Galleries are part of arbitrage in practice. Publishers have realized that if you can get the person that you paid just $0.05 to come through to your headline content to click through to other pages on your site on the same visit, you will still make $0.10 from the view of this second page; you've effectively spent $0 and make 100 per cent revenue on any additional pages visited by a user. That's why gallery-style pages are so popular – each time you slide beyond the first page, it's technically 100 per cent revenue per page for the publisher.

You spend $0.05 bringing someone through to your website, and you make $0.10 per page view, and the visitor clicks on three pages. So you'll make $0.30, minus $0.05 for media spend, so a profit of $0.25 per visit.

In summary:

- media spend per visitor – $0.05
- profit page 1 – 50 per cent ($0.05 profit)
- profit page 2 – 100 per cent ($0.10 profit)
- profit page 3 – 100 per cent ($0.10 profit)
- total profit per visitor – $0.25

The reason publishers can calculate this way comes down to how they get paid for their advertising – and how they buy their advertising in return. Most publishers get paid a CPM rate for the advertising eyeballs they generate. (CPM stands for cost per mille, or cost per thousand.)

This basically means that for every thousand views of an ad, a publisher will be paid $X amount. Know this and you can calculate, as above, what each visit to your site is worth. Get a visit and you are guaranteed this rate. But publishers, when they are looking to buy traffic to their website, don't buy a CPM view of their ad; they only pay for the actual click, buying on a cost-per-click (CPC) model and the corresponding visit to their website.

This means they are only 'paying for what they get', so there's no wasted spend from their side on advertising that doesn't correlate back to new visitors and ad revenue.

There's nothing wrong with this as a business model – it underpins a large swathe of digital publishing activity. Promoting your content to relevant audiences using paid methods is what every publisher should be looking to do in a competitive landscape.

The CPM acronym conundrum

CPM is one of the more commonly used acronyms in digital– if not the most common. It stands for cost per mille – that is, per thousand. It's the universal buy model for most digital advertising. The conundrum, of course, is why we use the Latin for thousand – mille. I can think of few other Latin acronyms in digital: for a forward-looking industry, devoid of tradition and very much a meritocracy, this inclusion is somewhat perplexing.

Clickbait

When the advertising rewards are so high and the business model blueprint behind it relatively easy to set up, execute and scale, as we've outlined above, there will always be those out to maximize returns and push boundaries. This is where 'clickbait' comes in. It is defined as:

> content whose main purpose is to attract attention and encourage visitors to click on a link to a particular webpage.

Now, every headline ever written was created with the purpose of attracting attention and to 'encourage visitors to click'. The clickbait term was hardly used five years ago; now it's fairly common parlance. But something many people forget is that clickbait has been around since the dawn of print media. When you think about it: what are newspaper headlines and magazine front covers if not a form of clickbait? It's nothing particularly new.

Consumers are used to it. They aren't stupid. They can smell an overly promotional headline or ridiculous hyperbole from miles away. But in a bid to maximize performance – remember, more visits equal more advertising money – increasingly many of the headlines you read online today go too far and can be misleading.

We've all seen them – titles that are so enticing that you cannot fail to click on them. They are often spur of the moment, such as, 'You wouldn't believe what Obama said to Trump on his last day in office'. Or they include imagery that really draws your attention: good-looking men and women; insinuating poses; photoshopped pics; shocking imagery – whatever it takes to draw you in.

Often the headline and the thumbnail image combine to pique your interest. A common ruse you may have seen are posts with titles such as '25 celebrities you didn't know were dead' – which run with an image of a celebrity that you are certain is still very much alive.

As consumers of content – always looking for a new story to share around the warm smartphone glow of the collective campfire – this sort of content naturally captures your interest. 'Oh, I didn't know they were dead,' is the natural response to make. So what do you do? You click on the headline, of course. And what happens then? Increasingly, you are let down. The expectation far outweighs the reality.

What we discover is that when you click through you are taken to a gallery page – and there is no mention of the celebrity used in the promotional thumbnail, just a list of celebrities that you are well aware have long since died. It's incorrect advertising, poor editorial, and fooling no one.

The clickbait value exchange

The value exchange for the consumer is terrible in this instance. It betrays the cardinal sin of advertising: it over-promises and under-delivers – which is the real issue, when the trade-off to the user's expectations of the quality of the content isn't matched with their perception of what's being offered.

While there really are millions of readers happy to be enticed by a thumbnail with a freakish picture or a claim about the questionable behaviour of high-profile celebs, the value exchange between reader expectation in most instances is far from the mark. That's the main problem. It's not the clickbait, as such; there's nothing wrong with trying to make a headline as click-able as possible. But when the headline doesn't live up to expectations, where is the benefit in that?

Fake news

While all publishers will be guilty of running clickbait, the same insatiable drive for impressions and the digital advertising revenue that underpins it is behind the growing level of fake news appearing online. It's the evolutionary leap from taking clickbait to a new level – or rather a new low – with the aim of generating more views for monetary gain.

The truth (as opposed to post-truth) of the situation is that, while there may be political motives behind some of the growth in fake news, the vast majority of fake news that is being published, promoted and shared across social media, content recommendation widgets and other promotional platforms has no political agenda whatsoever. It's created purely as clickbait, with the sole aim of driving as many eyeballs to a publication as possible and then maximizing the monetization of each visit.

Why report real news, when fake news is more entertaining?

Fake news has gained a lot of press in recent months. It first came to prominence on the back of Donald Trump's victory in the US election. Fake news was said to play a part in influencing swing voters; there were countless reports showing how Macedonian teenagers, employed as content writers, flooded social media with made-up stories.

We read about how we live in a post-truth world, where whoever shouts loudest is shouting the truth. It's very much on the radar of the media. Research by Brandwatch reported that from October 2016 to mid-January 2017, there were 54,000 media stories published with the phrase 'fake news' in the headline.[2]

The financial motivation behind fake news

Digital ad revenue is shoring up and promoting fake news. It's a sorry state of affairs. But it's true. The political aspect may draw the headlines, but it's often just a by-product of unscrupulous publications attempting to create fake news story 'hits' that resonate, get shares and drive considerable ad revenues their way.

Social media giants such as Facebook have had to react. Fake news does put platforms such as Facebook in a difficult position. How do you determine if something is 'fake' without establishing fact-checking credentials first? As Adam Mosseri, VP, News Feed, described in a press statement in December 2016: 'We [Facebook] believe in giving people a voice and that we cannot become arbiters of truth ourselves.'

Towards the end of 2016 Facebook announced a number of updates, such as easier reporting of suspect news, and tools for flagging disputed third-party stories. But it also stressed that it would look closely at how to disrupt the financial incentives for spammers. The press statement read:

> We've found that a lot of fake news is financially motivated. Spammers make money by masquerading as well-known news organizations, and posting hoaxes that get people to visit to their sites, which are often mostly ads. So we're doing several things to reduce the financial incentives.[3]

There will undoubtedly be more and more measures put in place across social media enterprises such as Facebook to minimize the threat that fake news poses in the months and years to come. It's an ongoing battle, but one that advertisers – those who spend billions across Facebook and social media – are watching closely.

'Tricksters, deceivers and manipulators'

Content recommendation providers have entered into the fake news debate, too, keen to highlight their stance. Adam Singolda, Founder and CEO of Taboola – which claims to be the largest content recommendation company on the planet, serving 12 billion recommendations a day to a billion people a month – in a blog post on the topic published 28 November 2016, shortly after Trump's election victory, reiterated what the company set out in their Advertiser Content Guidelines:

> Any type of fake content cannot and will not be tolerated on the Taboola network.[4]

The post lists many of the measures and processes that Taboola has in place to try and catch and filter out fake news, including the company's use of human content verification as opposed to an algorithm.

Singolda's post highlights another uncomfortable fact of life for the digital industry, though: whenever a new product, service or advertising format comes along, it is almost always targeted by unscrupulous 'tricksters, deceivers and manipulators' who 'inevitably appear to game every new advertising and distribution channel that emerges (very much like we witnessed with Search, and Display advertising 20 years ago).'

Cloakers

The Taboola post goes on to discuss 'cloakers' and how it can impact content recommendation widgets. Cloakers are advertisers who submit content that looks legitimate at first – so it passes the human verification process – but is then later replaced with fake content. To combat this Taboola launched Taboola Choice – a way for customers to report something that they don't like or that may be deceptive, fake or harmful.

Cloaking is just one example of the dubious practices employed by those out for profit at any cost. As Singolda concludes:

> Fake content is an industry-wide challenge. All of the largest online advertising and distribution companies are wrestling to find the solution to this ever-evolving cat-and-mouse game.

It's an interesting post; if you want to find out more you can read it at www. blog.taboola.com/fakenewspolicy.

Fake news, real problems

In November 2016, BuzzFeed News reported that fake election news stories generated more engagement on Facebook than election stories from a combined total of 19 major news publications, including the *New York Times*, *Washington Post*, NBC News and other reputable news sources.[5] The figures BuzzFeed quotes are astounding: 20 of the top-performing false election stories from hoax sites and hyperpartisan blogs generated 8,711,000 shares, reactions and comments on Facebook. The other news organizations generated 7,367,000 shares, reactions and comments on Facebook.

An additional poll conducted by Ipsos Public Affairs for BuzzFeed News in December 2016 found that as many as 75 per cent of American adults may believe fake news stories to be accurate.[6] The survey found that when Facebook is cited as a source of news, Americans are more likely to view the headlines as accurate. Chris Jackson from Ipsos argued that the 2016 presidential election in the US was significant as it 'may mark the point in modern political history when information and disinformation became a dominant electoral currency'.

Advertising fraud and bot traffic

Depending on what research you read, somewhere between 2 per cent, conservatively, and 90 per cent, drastically, of all online advertising is run fraudulently. This means it is advertising seen only by robots, scamming the measurement metrics and monetary advertising models and networks in place. It affects the entire industry. The presence of ad fraud is pervasive. It's difficult to root out because the vast majority of advertisers are not intentionally booking fraudulent campaigns; publishers are not actively seeking bot traffic when buying in traffic for publisher arbitrage; and no reputable technology company looks to partner with this type of advertising. But its presence persists.

The issue affects all digital advertising, including native advertising. Programmatic trading of advertising has in some ways made it easier for fraudsters to access the market – more inventory is available, more buyers are in the market for perceived high-performing inventory. Direct one-to-one relationships are rare – and the tactics fraudsters deploy are sophisticated:

mirroring legitimate sites and piggy-backing on inventory bought legitimately by traders is a common tactic. So you have to be ever vigilant for issues.

Sophisticated tools are increasingly being deployed to verify the authenticity of website traffic and many vendors adopt third-party tools such as Moat and Integral Ad Science to ensure that the impressions they serve against are real, and run on the digital properties they wanted to run against. But keeping one step ahead is a challenge.

All of the above are not the sole preserve of native advertising; they are far wider digital advertising trends and issues. They are deep-rooted problems that hit at the heart of the business of digital.

Some see native advertising as the white knight in this dark landscape, destined to clear the land and banish demons via cleaner ads, higher standards and more technical innovation to keep the bad guys at bay. Others see it as just another part of the darkness – a new tool that will inevitably be gamed, broken and utilized by unscrupulous people for financial gain.

Brand safety

Brand safety is an increasingly popular term in advertising. What does it mean? It is the phrase used to describe the very real concern that brands have about the environment in which their advertising is seen and being run. It's become more and more prevalent as digital advertising spend has increased and automation and programmatic modes of buying have become more popular. Programmatic's mantra is typically: you buy audience, not site.

The argument goes that with ever more detailed targeting capabilities and automated tools, it's possible to serve your advertising to the right people, wherever they are. This is true, as we see throughout this book: digital advertising's strength is in its ability to filter, target and serve relevant advertising based on user data. But there are concerns. Rightly, brands are worried that their advertising – when run across the internet – is going to appear next to content and on websites that are inappropriate.

There have been countless examples where brand safety has been breached in the past: banner advertising appearing on pornographic sites; video advertising appearing before or during dubious video content; retargeting campaigns appearing next to sensitive or inappropriate news content. It's a genuine concern for advertisers around how and where they place their advertising budgets.

In the UK there was something of an advertiser backlash in early 2017. It began with an investigation published by *The Times* in February, which claimed digital advertising was inadvertently funding terrorism.[7] The article claimed that some of 'the world's biggest brands are unwittingly funding Islamic extremists, white supremacists and pornographers by advertising on their websites'. Programmatic digital advertising was cited as the main culprit, and the article went on to claim that 'blacklists designed to prevent digital adverts from appearing next to it are not fit for purpose'. The article drew front-page headlines and even raised questions in parliament, putting brand safety very much front of mind for brands.

In March 2017 the brand safety issue escalated in the UK as numerous advertisers, including one of the world's leading media buying agencies, Havas, withdrew all of their digital advertising spend in the UK with Google over brand safety fears. Havas reportedly pulled their advertising spend after they claimed Google had been 'unable to provide specific reassurances, policy and guarantees that their video or display content is classified either quickly enough or with the correct filters'.[8]

Brand safety is a wide digital advertising challenge. It's part of the same issues we've discussed in this chapter already. The question that brand safety raises is: can you have scale with quality? Can you buy cheap and be sure you are not risking your brand reputation by placing your advertising in the darker corners of the web? Places where, admittedly, some of your customers can be found at times: but do you want to be serving them advertising while they are there?

Digital advertising

Contributed by Damian Ryan, author of *Understanding Digital Marketing* and a partner in the Moore Stephens corporate finance team

Advertisers and media owners are now learning what 'responsible' looks like. The price of ignoring the interests of consumers is starting to tot up. What began as a sort of polite shrug in the direction of privacy and respect of data is now making its way down the corridor to the boardroom.

Responsible marketers are now asking much better questions of media owners:

- How do I know this traffic is real – are these humans engaging with my ad or robots?

- Where did you get this data from – is it compliant with GDPR (General Data Protection Regulation)?
- How do I know you won't position my ad next to something unsavoury?

The recent exodus of brands from YouTube is what responsible looks like. Consumers are getting it too – they don't like being forced into engaging with noisy, irresponsible advertisers. The rise of ad blocking is a clear vote in the direction of what our beloved Internet marketplace needs to be.

Safe to do business. Safe to engage. Value for time and value for money. I believe the next phase of the internet will be victorious for those brands who realize TRUST is the commercial advantage, and invest to build and protect trust.

Native advertising and brand safety

Brand safety is not guaranteed with native advertising, but it is easier to ensure your brand advertising only runs on sites that you want it to run against. If you opt to run brand content publisher partnerships with respected brands, you can largely expect your brand to be safe on these sites.

Likewise, the majority of existing in-feed distribution native advertising platforms offer high levels of transparency to advertisers too. We offer scale by working with a multitude of publishers, but crucially, we maintain direct working relationships with our publishers. We review their sites continually. We work with them in partnership to improve brand safety. We block pages that are inappropriate for advertising, for example, and implement stringent keyword and category block-lists.

Likewise, when buying inventory programmatically, it's possible to share all domain referrer information, too. So buyers know where their advertising has run. In addition, many native providers and publishers looking to package their native inventory programmatically for buyers can create private marketplace (PMP) deals on agreed website URLs.

These measures mean that native advertisers and their partners can more accurately guarantee against inappropriate brand safety environments.

The native advertising challenge

This is the environment in which native advertising lives. Fake news, click-bait, ad fraud and brand safety are real challenges for the digital industry, and native advertising faces these challenges, too, if it wants to maintain its legitimacy and effectiveness.

There are limits to using content as an advertising currency – particularly when it is gamed by the unscrupulous. This content failure is leaving millions of readers disillusioned, which, for a format built on the distribution of content, is a serious issue for native advertising. These practices devalue the work of social media platforms, native technology businesses and publishers everywhere: if advertisers lose trust in these native advertising products, the success of the format is inevitably in question.

These digital issues don't just undermine platforms, or devalue the work of premium publishers with a heritage of thorough journalism and exacting reporting standards; they do more than that. They shrink their advertising revenue. They eat into the advertising budgets that marketers could be spending with publications that champion good-quality journalism.

Instead, money ends up being diverted towards media properties that are nothing more than pages of advertising, populated with content that at best is inaccurate, at worst is knowingly false. Powered by people who at best are entrepreneurial-minded digital people looking to get ahead, but at worst are involved in sophisticated organized crime or terrorism. What this means is that the ad revenue available to premium publishers falls, and with it the resources open to these publications to invest in quality journalism.

Writing in *MediaPost* in July 2015, Ari Rosenberg, Founder of IPC Pricing – a company set up with the aim to 'fix how advertising is priced and sold so incentives between advertisers and publishers are more aligned and consumers see better ads' – described the modern digital publishing landscape: 'Today, the circle of competition for online dollars has grown so large for traditional publishers... publishers are battling against competition they can't see.' He went on to describe how this competition has a far more detrimental effect on traditional media publications – the big name publishers that are household names – because 'premium publishers expend energy and resources to obtain, nurture and hold consumer attention — while ad dollars get awarded to sites that are better at losing it.'[9]

Native advertising is not the solution to these issues: the issue of achieving the dizzying scale that digital promises, with no potential pitfalls; the challenge of reaching your target audience – and only your target audience – and only in the environment and digital 'neighbourhoods' you see as appropriate for your brand. These are monumental tasks that the advertising industry is currently grappling with. Native advertising, depending on your viewpoint, is part of the problem yet simultaneously part of the solution. Once again, it falls to being 'all things to all men'.

But as these legitimate concerns grow, in the near future, we may begin to see the long anticipated 'flight to quality'. Advertisers – and the technology they use – will become ever more rigorous in filtering out inappropriate brand environments and the unscrupulous gaming of the system. Native advertising will undoubtedly be part of this move to quality.

A publisher's view of native advertising

Contributed by Piers North, Strategy Director, Trinity Mirror

You can look back at the period of around 2011 as the dawn of the phenomenon of native advertising. The increasing consumer shift to mobile, as well as the increased automation of media buying and the arrival of Facebook on the advertising scene, created the conditions for the beginning of its march to dominance.

Purists will argue, with some legitimacy, that native really arrived in the form of search marketing back in the late 1990s – paid-for search results were the ultimate form of ads mirroring the form and function of their environment. So-called 'display' has really spent 20 years dragging itself into the native arena.

Now that native has arrived in the non-search arena, its rise seems unstoppable. More and more mobile consumption means that traditional ad formats are becoming increasingly challenged.

It would be wrong to say that native is completely divorced from its traditional cousin and something completely of a different world, though. It is still just advertising, and some native formats are only marginally different from their predecessors. But the ability to run across all devices, the increasing simplicity of the creative, the better engagement rates and the ability for the ads to act as a content marketing distribution tool in their own right or a traditional broadcast and performance message is marking native out as the Swiss army knife of digital advertising.

As such, native advertising, along with video, will be the two big drivers for publishers in the next few years. Native provides solutions for their mobile monetization challenge as well as driving performance and scale for their content marketing solutions.

That is not to say native advertising, in itself, will be a lifeline for traditional content businesses. The same challenges that have disrupted publishers in the standard display business model don't disappear overnight; low yields, audience over context buying and the overly complex ad tech value chain to name a few. But native does at least allow a framework on which to try and build a content-led business for the future.

Endnotes

1 Outbrain Case Study (2017) [online] www.outbrain.com/case-studies/edb [accessed 23 May 2017]

2 Benes, R (23 January 2017) The global state of fake news in 5 charts [online] http://digiday.com/media/fake-news-charts/ [accessed 28 March 2017]

3 Mosseri, A (15 December 2016) News Feed FYI: Addressing hoaxes and fake news [online] http://newsroom.fb.com/news/2016/12/news-feed-fyi-addressing-hoaxes-and-fake-news/ [accessed 28 March 2017]

4 Siingolda, A (28 November 2016) Fake news is everyone's business – and our responsibility [online] http://blog.taboola.com/fakenewspolicy/ [accessed 28 March 2017]

5 Silverman, C (16 November 2016) This analysis shows how viral fake election news stories outperformed real news on Facebook [online] www.buzzfeed.com/craigsilverman/viral-fake-election-news-outperformed-real-news-on-facebook [accessed 28 March 2017]

6 Silverman, C (7 December 2016) Most Americans who see fake news believe it, new survey says [online] www.buzzfeed.com/craigsilverman/fake-news-survey [accessed 28 March 2017]

7 Mostrous, A (9 February 2017) Big brands fund terror through online adverts [online] www.thetimes.co.uk/article/big-brands-fund-terror-knnxfgb98 [accessed 28 March 2017]

8 Grierson, J, Topping, A and Sweney, M (17 March 2017) French advertising giant pulls out of Google and YouTube [online] www.theguardian.com/media/2017/mar/17/google-pledges-more-control-for-brands-over-ad-placement [accessed 28 March 2017]

9 Rosenberg, A (2 July 2015) *Media Post*, It's an arbitrage media world – premium publishers just die in it [online] http://www.mediapost.com/publications/article/253192/its-an-arbitrage-media-world-premium-publisher.html [accessed 28 March 2017]

The rise of the content studio   13

You do not have to look far into the world of content marketing and native advertising before coming across the content studio. Content studios, or content labs, are increasingly the engine rooms behind a lot of brand-owned content marketing and branded content native advertising campaigns. They are the commercial content arms of leading publishers such as the *New York Times*, the *Atlantic*, the *Guardian*, the *Telegraph*, Trinity Mirror, *The Economist*, Quartz, the *Financial Times*, and many, many more.

In fact, almost every large publication will have a bespoke content studio, dedicated to working on branded content solutions for clients. As an example of this growth, MediaRadar found more than 1,000 sites selling native advertising in 2017, up from 218 publisher sites in 2015.[1]

Their aim? To provide creative content solutions and create award-winning branded content for some of the world's leading brands. The best content studios instinctively understand the commercial content space. They are comfortable adopting the content marketing mantra of 'think like a publisher', because they are publishers: the majority of the staff within content studios often hail from editorial and storytelling backgrounds.

This means they are never short of ideas for what will resonate with the readers of their publication. But perhaps more importantly for a brand, they know how to go about creating this content too – and all with the flair you would expect from an experienced newsroom team. They have the specific skills needed to create exciting story-led advertising.

This has been something publishers have always had access to, haven't they? So, you could ask, why the need to create these content studios? Why now?

The reason is economics. And perception. In the past a brand (and the publisher sales rep) wanting the input of an editorial resource knew it was an uphill battle. 'Church' and 'state' were completely separate. Editors tasked with writing advertorials thought it beneath them on many occasions. It wasn't their job to do this. Or so they thought. But as native advertising has grown – and content solutions now significantly underpin the digital revenues of major publications – the case for independent commercial content teams has grown. The market for story-led advertising that delivers deep engagement with your target audience continues to increase. It is the future. As a result, more and more publishers recognize the need to invest in their commercial content capabilities; hence the rise in the content studio.

Dedicated commercial content teams

By splitting out newsrooms into content studios, it reinforces to brands and their agencies that publishers have a dedicated team ready to work on their commercial briefs: rather than commercial content languishing somewhere within newsrooms as an editorial afterthought.

But what is a content studio, really, though? Is it a creative agency, or is it a newsroom? Does it create editorial or does it create ads? Is it a genuine challenge to the age-old agency–client relationship, or a complement to it that adds value for brand and agency? The answer depends on the content studio, their resource and the overall business objectives behind it.

The very best content studios are all of the above. They are creative agencies that understand the newsroom and editorial processes: they create editorial, but they also create advertising – usually at the same time. They understand the need for agencies in the client–media matrix, rather than resenting agency input. The best work together with stakeholders to give their creative capability the business nous required to turn an idea into a commercial reality.

Scaling the content studio

The commercial content studio is still a relatively new phenomenon. Most studios are less than five years old in their current operations. Publishers have invested heavily and promoted extensively these entities as significant digital innovations. Some would have you believe they are the 'silver bullet' solution to dwindling publishing revenue.

But is there a downside? The downside to maintaining all of this content expertise is that it is expensive. Whether you are creating editorial content for consumers, or commercial content for a brand, the process of creating content that is actually good, that someone will find interesting, usually takes a lot of time. The problem with things that take time is that it is difficult to scale; and scale is everything in digital.

Maintaining expensive in-house staff – who are tasked with not just creating new and entertaining content, campaign to campaign, but are also juggling all the various sign-offs, re-works and approvals that content-led advertising goes through – is demanding. Plus, when you have major brands and agencies creating amazing multimedia brand content, the bar is set extremely high for the calibre of work an advertiser will expect to see from a publisher's content studio in return. Expensive multimedia content and videography can quickly eat away at margin.

Extending content reach

Then we have the issue of reach when it comes to distributing the content: most publications fail to get the necessary 'organic' reach that their advertisers expect from the amount of money they are spending. So what this means is that invariably many publishers extend their reach by purchasing additional traffic – or eyeballs – from content recommendation, social media and in-feed native distribution providers, usually on a cost-per-click basis. This gets them the audience reach they require to make the campaign a success – but the media spend for this activity comes from their margin. Plus, most savvy marketing agencies know that they could buy the same activity from the same providers for lower rates than what the publisher is paying for the same product.

All of this potentially leaves publishers in a jam: profit margins can be squeezed significantly by the twin costs of creative build and distribution.

The changing economics of the content studio

You need a lot of high-paying work to maintain a high-calibre creative team. Agencies have known this for years. Which is why most of them work on a retainer basis with their clients. This gives them a better ability to manage incoming revenue, which is key for planning things such as how many staff you can afford to hire. Some publishers, such as *The Times* and Hearst Digital, are reportedly trying to charge some clients on a retainer basis, but the vast majority of content studios in existence today are funded along a campaign-to-campaign basis. This is extremely challenging to scale. Not all publishers will be able to do this. Those publishers that do so will increasingly come to resemble content agencies in terms of their make-up, attitude and financial model.

Interview with Michael Villaseñor, Creative Director, Ad Marketing and Innovation at the *New York Times*

Michael Villaseñor is an award-winning creative director who is passionate about challenging the status quo of user experience and advertising. The convergence of creative thinking, emerging technology, and clean, simple design aesthetic are all embraced for every project that lands on his desk.

How would you describe native advertising in one sentence?

Native advertising is the creation of brand opportunities within a digital environment that embrace the surrounding user experience and interface, creating a seamless integration.

The user experience is similar: for example, a video that plays in the stream the same way that an editorial video would; but the layout includes labels and visual cues, such as differentiating background colours or fonts, to create contrast between the advertisement and the editorial content.

Do you like the term native advertising?

I think that labelling something as 'native advertising' creates an unusual separation between it and 'the rest' of advertising. I appreciate looking at advertising as 'more native' versus 'less native', in which the distinction is made by whether the creative embraces more of the brand identity versus more of the host site or experience.

Why do you think native advertising has become so successful?

Native advertising has been successful because of a few core components, including but not limited to:

- the ability to work within restrictive environments, not being limited to the gutters of the page or standard sizes;
- native's ability to integrate the style of a given page and provide an integrated experience within the larger environment.

You work for a prestigious news organization – what do you say to those who claim native advertising blurs the boundaries between 'church' and 'state'?

The *New York Times* maintains a strong belief of clear separation of what content is created by the newsroom versus what content is created by T

Brand Studio. Our readers' trust is by far the most important aspect of what we do. Branded content shouldn't be positioned to confuse the reader or deteriorate that trust we maintain with our readership.

From a creative point of view, what do you like about native advertising as a format?

I appreciate the restrictive nature of the native format. In many ways the restrictions create a bigger opportunity for designers to create original, beautiful work that shares a visual language across the entire site experience.

How do you approach mobile from a creative point of view?

Creative for mobile has largely suffered from the attempt to port over existing methods for desktop onto the smaller form factor. How we've been approaching it at the *New York Times* is to consider methods of how advertising can be 'integrated', from the consideration of design, utility and shared user experience. Always labelled clearly, mobile advertising can begin to play an active role within the stream versus a disruptive one.

What has been your most successful piece of native advertising?

I think in a lot of ways we've found great success with the 'paid post' model. Not only does it provide a large canvas for advertisers to showcase original brand stories in a voice that T Brand Studio creates, but it's also completely respectful of and clear to the reader that it is a paid opportunity.

Do you think agencies and brands really 'get' native content?

They do, and in the last two years I've observed a marked improvement and flexibility of how the concept comes to life. In a way this has largely been manifested through branded video content that T Brand Studio has created.

What skills do you think are needed to work as a native advertising content creator?

In order to be an effective editor in brand advertising, a background in writing, preferably journalism, is preferred. Many of our editors come with extensive backgrounds in writing for top name publishers, providing our brands with original work that is of the highest calibre.

What do you see as the future of native advertising over the next 10 years?

The future of native advertising will continue to shape and shift based on the evolvement of the platform and web framework. Considering that native formats have been around since print was the only medium and that they continue to evolve as reader habits do, they aren't going anywhere. However, I could imagine a native future where we evolve the current full-page model to something more integrated and bite-sized, which can be consumed in a variety of ways and used on a wider range of platforms.

Endnote

1   Moses, L (9 March 2017) 'The model can't hold': Publishers face content studio growing pains [online] http://digiday.com/media/model-cant-hold-publishers-face-content-studio-growing-pains/ [accessed 28 March 2017]

Objections to native advertising

14

No book about native advertising would be complete without admitting that it has its detractors. In some circles, the phrase, when uttered, is tantamount to the very worst type of swear word.

Why do they object to native advertising?

There are those in publishing circles who see native advertising as a wolf in sheep's clothing: something to be fought off at all costs, let alone encouraged. Detractors of the format see native advertising as fundamentally pulling away one of the key tenets of publishing: editorial independence. What is popularly referred to in publishing circles as the separation of church from state, or editorial teams from advertising teams.

Speak to an editor that retired pre-millennium and you quickly realize that print editors spent the majority of their careers blissfully unaware of the commercial dealings that underpinned their salaries: their job was to simply think about their intended audience and go about creating content that would appeal to that audience. Of course, the editor knew what headlines and front pages translated into more newspaper sales, but even they normally didn't know what readership figures specific advertisers were looking for. KPIs and performance metrics, reader engagement and the like were completely unknown.

Conversely, the advertising teams had little to no idea what many editorial teams were going to run with on any given day – especially within daily newspaper publishing. Detractors of native advertising argue that this 'native advertising' business is blurring the lines between the two, which means that the integrity of a publication is at risk if it loses its perception as an impartial teller of stories. But an even greater risk, many argue, is that native advertising could damage the reputation of publishing as a whole.

When it's difficult to tell if something is a freely written, impartial piece of journalism, or a piece of content written by, or on behalf of, a brand with a commercial objective behind it, trust becomes difficult. Whether the content is good or not is not the point; the motive behind its creation can warp a reader's view, and taint not just the trust in that particular publication, but consumer trust in everything that they read.

Contributed by: Daniel Emery, journalist and ex-BBC Technology Correspondent

Print publishing is dying a death; you need to break even to continue to exist as a publisher. There are many commercial factors continually at play: native advertising, commercial content and digital as a whole are just part of the situation. When you reach a position, such as where the *Guardian* is asking readers for donations, you know that's not a sustainable business model.

In the past advertisers did advertising, journalists did journalism. Now it's literally a 360 soup: marketing, PR, advertising, journalism, social, etc. And creating 'stuff' for this gets called 'content' and that covers a pretty wide range.

In some respects it's a golden age for content publishing, but it is also a poisoned chalice. You can create content and reach audiences far more easily today. Digital and social have removed the content gatekeepers (journalists). But everyone is doing that, too, so you have to be more creative to get what you want to say out there.

Everyone is producing content – and there's no demarcation between what is journalism and what isn't. As it stands, we are seeing the slow death of traditional journalism. Resources are getting thinner; journalists do not have time to fact-check like they used to. We increasingly live in an age of 'churnilism', where news content is regurgitated from newswire copy, Google News trends and Facebook trending articles and repeated verbatim ad infinitum.

Is this journalism 'selling' its soul in the face of a changing commercial pressure? How do you separate truth from fiction in this scenario? The demand for information and content has not diminished in the digital age. The choice is almost infinite today, but there are simply no checks and balances to see if any of the content we are consuming is true or not.

When 85% of all advertising budgets go to just two businesses – Facebook and Google – and you have the rest of the media industry scrambling around trying to grab what is left of the rest, you can see how and why expensive commodities such as fact-checking and investigative journalism are in decline. Is it the generational decline of news? Possibly. If Google or Facebook step into the news creation fray – instead of remaining as they are today as giant newsagents – it would change the dynamic dramatically.

Will this happen? Who knows? As it stands, the future is pretty dark. Society needs to work out if it prefers to have a few extra quid in its pocket by accessing news for free, or be informed.

John Oliver and native advertising

In a now famous segment from August 2014, which was dedicated exclusively to native advertising – and counterintuitively did much to popularize the term – British comedian John Oliver, on his HBO show *Last Week Tonight with John Oliver*, described native advertising as 'repurposed bovine waste'.[1] He also described how even the very best examples of native advertising were 'like listening to the one Katy Perry song you like'. What he meant by that is: even though this is OK, you know there's a lot better music – or content, in the native advertising example – out there that you could be listening to.

Andrew Sullivan, journalist, blogger and media commentator, writing on his blog in January 2013, highlighted the commercial and moral conundrum:

> I have nothing but admiration for innovation in advertising and creative revenue-generation online. Without it, journalism will die. But if advertorials become effectively indistinguishable from editorial, aren't we in danger of destroying the village in order to save it?[2]

Is native advertising a convenient term to use to bash modern publishing?

It's worth noting that there is a wider theme at play here. Many objections are not necessarily directed against native advertising, per se, but directed at the far broader influence of advertising in light of ongoing commercial pressures at publishers, and the blurring of these lines between editorial and advertising.

Native advertising in the past has been the convenient 'catch-all' term they often use. In 2014 the then BBC journalist Robert Peston described the term native advertising as an 'Orwellian newspeak-like phrase'.[3] It sums up the editorial objections that native advertising has faced to gain acceptance. For people that have spent their lives reporting, writing journalism, producing and broadcasting, native advertising is a symbol of commercial meddling in areas where it should not be allowed.

Now that native advertising has matured as a medium, grown in popularity and in many ways become a part of the everyday media consumption habits of consumers, have these concerns disappeared?

There may be fewer blog posts voicing concerns than there were in the past, but this is largely as a result of editorial folk retreating into acceptance in the wake of the commercial realities in existence today. It doesn't necessarily mean they now suddenly like all things native advertising related. It's a begrudging acceptance of the way it is.

But publishers themselves have done a lot of work to maintain the distinction between church and state since native advertising has grown:

- New departments, such as Guardian Labs, the NYT T Brand Studio, the *Telegraph*'s Spark and countless others, have been created, populated with commercial journalists with the sole aim of creating commercial content (see Chapter 13, The Rise of the Content Studio).

- Publishers have split out the publishing process for commercial content, too. Instead of lumping all content, commercial and non-commercial content, and publishing via a publisher's in-house content management system (CMS), most major publishers have divorced the process and work with native tech providers directly so that commercial teams publish content to their sites themselves, without having to use an in-house CMS, or badger editorial teams to do it for them. This effectively silos the different content and breaks up responsibility for publication between editorial and commercial teams.

- Better labelling: as the market has matured, a greater uniformity and improved best practice examples – across publications and the industry as a whole – are leading to better processes being put in place.

- Better units: many publishers are adopting slight adjustments to their native advertising units to offer some subtle differences between advertiser content and editorial content. Points such as adding shading around advertiser content units, greater emphasis on highlighting the advertising disclosure, as well as the adoption of the universal ad choices logo, which consumers recognize as relating to advertising, help reiterate the point that what they are seeing is an advertisement. This has eased many objections.

The digital advertising industry as a whole is also playing its part. Brands themselves continue to create some truly engaging content that is less about the 'hard sell' and more about genuinely informing their target audience. When this is done well, objections diminish.

Native advertising is here to stay, and – as we've explained in this book – is going to flourish. It's the future. If publishers are going to survive, it is down to them to work closely with advertisers to create good native advertisements that meet this audience expectation.

There is a major boom in content marketing among brands, of which native advertising is very much a part. But what this also means is that publishers are no longer the only conduit of information. Brands can speak directly to their customers if they choose. But they still want to work with leading publishers. Why? Because they have audience, legitimacy and trust.

What are the main objections to native advertising among publishers?

I've lost count of the number of times I've pitched our native advertising technology to publishers. In the early days, when native advertising was still in its infancy – and knowledge of what, even, the phrase meant was limited – we spent a lot of time running through the mechanics of our native advertising offering with publishers, and explaining exactly how it worked. Big or small, whatever the publisher, whenever objections were raised, we could almost always break them down to the below.

Disclosure/labelling

Publishers are very concerned by labelling and the disclosure that surrounds their advertising. So they should be: it's their legal responsibility to ensure that advertising is labelled correctly as just that – advertising – but also to ensure that nothing is lost by the user experience when implementing native advertising. No native advertising company, publisher, advertiser or technology provider should want to run native advertising without proper disclosure in place. Not only is it the law in most countries, there's also really no benefit in trying to dupe a consumer into clicking on an ad they don't think is an ad and do not want to see. There's no benefit for the publisher in doing that, but there's really no benefit for an advertiser, either. If you are promoting good content that you've created as a brand, you should be happy to run it with your name on it – and with full disclosure in place that the content you are promoting is paid for.

Disclosure: the must-have for all native advertising

While native advertising is designed to mimic the look and feel of the editorial or content around it, it should not be taken that native advertising in any way is designed to 'fool' consumers into interacting with the ads. The vast majority of native advertising that you interact with is labelled: no publisher, social platform or technology vendor worth anything would consider running native advertising without any form of disclosure in place.

Most native ads are labelled as either 'promoted by', 'sponsored by' or simply 'advertising by', or some other similar definition depending on the publisher and/or the type of native ad product running on their website. While there have been a few high-profile cases of native advertising falling foul of regulators, for an industry growing so fast – and constantly innovating – by and large the market does a good job at self-regulation.

There is no benefit for you as a business if you try to not fully disclose the fact that you are promoting paid-for content. You should be proud to label the content as your own. Not only does this offer clear disclosure and build consumer trust, but it's also great branding for you and your business: remember, not everyone will click on your ads – but everyone scrolling through the feed where your ads appear will see and read the headline – and your brand prominently displayed as the originator.

Don't think about disclosure, just recognize that you need to have it, and leave the rest to the publishers and native ad platforms that you work with to put in place. Your time is far better spent coming up with great content-led marketing ideas.

Positioning of the native advertising unit

This is often a difficult objection to overcome with certain publishers. After explaining how native advertising works – and highlighting especially how the modern digital eco-system is all about the feed – and how advertisers are increasingly looking for access to it, we were often left aghast when it came to integrate a publisher and their response would be: 'Can you integrate into the display units?'

It was as if all the benefits of native advertising had fallen on deaf ears. These publishers wanted the new revenue opportunity, but they didn't want to change anything on their side to benefit from it. It was frustrating.

It was only after holding a frank conversation with one publisher that I realized some of the issues publishers face in 'selling in' native advertising internally. I remember the call well. I expressed my exasperation with the publisher for suggesting we integrate into a banner slot on a category page. I suggested another slot – an existing content unit that was in-feed, above the fold, surrounded by other editorial units. It was perfect for our type of native advertising – and I knew it would perform well for the publisher there, increasing the revenue we could pay them considerably as a result. The publisher sighed. There was a long pause, and then he said:

> Dale, I'll level with you. I've spent the last three years arguing with the editorial director here and the entire business executive about the commercial team 'owning' the right-hand rail of this category page. We agreed that this was my slot for advertising, editorial have the rest. This is why I am trying to integrate you into this unit.' He paused a bit longer and sighed once more. 'And now you want me to go back to the editor and tell him I want one of his editorial units too?' Just before he hung up, he repeated in exasperation, 'Three years.'

The above conversation illustrates some of the issues faced internally across publishers when trying to integrate third-party native advertising. It took some time – and a few meetings on my part with the editor – but we did subsequently integrate this publisher into in-feed native advertising positions. They remain a key publishing partner of ours.

Editorial objections

As the above illustrates, editorial teams can be hostile to native advertising. All but the most naive of editors can, in today's publishing environment, though, fail to recognize the commercial necessity faced by many publications in adopting native advertising. As the champions of what their audiences want to see, purveyors of content and user experience, it's easy to see why editorial teams raise objections. At some publications it's the editorial team that wear the trousers; at others, what the commercial team wants, happens. Neither are ideal. The trick is in finding the right balance for editor, advertiser and user.

The blurring of the lines between editorial and advertiser is always a potential barrier to native advertising. But as I've set out above, better labelling and understanding, clear disclosure and better measures by publishers to divorce internally the creation of commercial content and the distribution of that content generally mitigate these concerns.

Advertising control

This is always a concern among publishers when integrating third-party demand: how do you ensure that the advertisers and their advertising messages remain appropriate to your audience? The same question comes up if you are a display advertising network, video network or provider of native advertising, but in my experience, publishers have greater concerns around inappropriate native advertising appearing on their site than many other forms of advertising. Why? This is a compliment to native advertising as a format: publishers care more, because they, like their website visitors, actually notice the native advertising that is running on their websites. Display networks, for example, suffer from banner blindness. Maintaining control of what ads appear to your users is obviously of paramount importance to publishers – and native advertising has the exact same safety measures you'd expect from other formats. Advertiser blacklists, topic blocks, domain blocking, IAB category blocks, are all commonly put in place, as well as pre-approval of all advertising if necessary by more stringent publishers.

The value of publishers

The real value of leading publishers to brand advertisers is that they have engaged audiences and a reputation for authority. No one wants prestigious publishers to lose that prestige. From an advertising perspective it could be a disaster. The very media that brands are looking to advertise in would be devalued to an extent that they would be seen as irrelevant. There is a trust among readers of quality newspapers – with over a century of print heritage – that any new digital publishing start-up, or brand, just does not have.

At the heart of publisher success is maintaining this authority and the editorial integrity of publisher editorial teams in the face of ongoing commercial pressure. It's not an easy task. It's important that publishers continue to think like publishers and that brands don't use their considerable spend to change the news. There are responsibilities on both sides.

The 'click culture' of chasing online visitors is something that brands, their agencies, trade bodies and ad tech vendors across the digital divide are keen to address – and have been debating for a very long time about how to implement. Publishers are no different and are part of the solution that will come. If done right, native advertising is a financial boon to publishers that will allow them to flourish – and invest in editorial integrity – for many years to come.

Endnotes

1 Wemple, E (4 August 2014) Native advertising is repurposed bovine waste [online] www.washingtonpost.com/blogs/erik-wemple/wp/2014/08/04/hbos-john-oliver-native-advertising-is-repurposed-bovine-waste/?utm_term=.d33fb35dd0d9 [accessed 25 May 2017]

2 Sullivan, A (21 February 2013) Guess which BuzzFeed piece is an ad [online] http://dish.andrewsullivan.com/threads/enhanced-advertorial-techniques/#bf2 [accessed 28 March 2017]

3 Guardian Staff (6 June 2014) Robert Peston's speech warns of threat to journalism from native ads – full text [online] www.theguardian.com/media/2014/jun/06/robert-peston-threat-journalism-native-ads-charles-wheeler-lecture-full-text [accessed 28 March 2017]

PART FIVE
The future of
native advertising

Programmatic native advertising 15

As we've outlined in earlier sections of this book, there are distinct types of native advertising in existence. For brands, they are not mutually exclusive – and all of them have their distinct benefits and advantages.

But perhaps nothing has more potential – and is potentially as controversial – in the native advertising space today than the adoption of programmatic native advertising. Like native advertising itself, it's a challenge and an opportunity.

What is programmatic advertising?

Before we look at programmatic native advertising, let's look a little at what programmatic advertising actually is. Programmatic in relation to the advertising/marketing arena is the process by which advertising is bought and sold via the use of software. Or, as Digiday put it in their introduction to all things programmatic, *WTF is Programmatic?*, 'It's using machines to buy ads, basically.'[1]

Programmatic allows advertisers and media owners a platform to build economies of scale via sophisticated bidding systems. The buying and selling process is largely automated – a lot of programmatic advertising operates via real-time bidding (RTB), so trades are immediate and ongoing. The entire system is underpinned by sophisticated technology, platforms and innovative processes. It's revolutionized and disrupted digital advertising in recent years to an enormous extent and set the entire industry along a road we know not where it will lead. But the changes are swift and irreversible.

The buying and selling advertising landscape of 2030 will be so fundamentally different from the ad landscape that existed in 2000 that it will be like comparing modern life with the Bronze Age. Change is rapid. The best comparison I can find to describe the sheer magnitude of the changes programmatic and automation are bringing to advertising is what happened in the finance industry a generation before. The financial markets were transformed in the 1980s and early 1990s by rapid changes in trading technology. Old-style 'trading pits' were replaced predominantly by software that allowed far more accuracy, volume and guarantees. Something similar is happening in advertising trading today. Programmatic advertising is, effectively, similar to trading stocks and shares today, just with advertising.

In February 2017, Kyle Brierley, Director of Media and Revenue Strategy at Business.com, described programmatic trading along financial trading lines:

> Programmatic buying is actually very simple, and is almost identical to the stock market. The value of each share is determined by the law of scarcity, and more importantly by a simple supply/demand curve. The same laws exist for media inventory.[2]

In March 2017 a pilot service was launched with the aim of creating a 'futures' market for advertising, using the same technology as the financial markets. The New York Interactive Advertising Exchange (Nyiax) released to a small private pilot audience. Nyiax operates on a combination of Nasdaq's trading architecture and blockchain technology.

The industry is going through a process of enormous change in how advertising is bought and sold. Native advertising is now very much a part of this process.

Native advertising goes programmatic

Programmatic trading initially only disrupted digital banner display and video trading. These were the first ad products to move to programmatic. Until very recently native advertising was not programmatically traded. Why? The main reason was down to numbers. The number 2.3 to be precise. Confused? You probably will be, but let me explain in brief:

Until the adoption of the OpenRTB 2.3 protocol, it was impossible to run a native advertising campaign via a programmatic platform. The problem was the moving parts that go into a native ad, in comparison with banner ads and video, for example. A banner, when traded programmatically, is typically one simple script – one line of code you load into the programmatic platform and away you go, buying ad space programmatically for your banners. But what do you do when you essentially need to load in a title, description, image and disclosure into these platforms? From a tech point of view, that's potentially three or four different pieces of data that need to go into one ad. Programmatic platforms were not built to do this. Until the US IAB's Real-Time Bidding (RTB) Project – the OpenRTB 2.3 specification – was introduced to provide support and standardization for the industry around native ads. This all happened in 2015. Today programmatic native advertising is big business. Much of the predicted growth in native advertising spend outlined in Chapter 5 (The global native advertising market) is driven by programmatic native advertising.

The in-feed distribution tier outlined in Chapter 6 (The different types of native advertising) is largely powered by programmatic native advertising. Why? Programmatic promises automation and the standardization of buying and selling, reducing workload on publishers and advertisers. It also often pits native advertising against display advertising when it comes to performance: and when click-through rates (CTR) and performance metrics are compared like for like, native advertising usually wins – so you see more and more ad spend move from display into native advertising as a result.

In March 2017, Nativo announced an integration with programmatic demand-side platform (DSP) The Trade Desk. It means that the Nativo True Native format – which is similar to the publisher partnership branded content native advertising offering, which allows sponsored content to remain on a publisher's site instead of clicking out to a branded landing page – is available to trade programmatically for the first time.[3]

It's an innovative move that is just one example of how technology businesses in the native space are making native advertising available programmatically. It's a trend that is going to continue as programmatic buying becomes the normal way to buy advertising in the years ahead.

Google and native advertising

Earlier in this book we demonstrated the impressive growth that native advertising has enjoyed in recent years. For technology businesses that have done much to power this growth, it has meant considerable success – and over the next number of years this success is on course to increase substantially. Programmatic native advertising is a key part of this growth and will lay the foundations for its success. Momentum appears to be with native advertising, particularly on mobile.

Little wonder, then, that the biggest player in digital is now looking very carefully at the native advertising space. But it was only in 2016 that Google announced its native advertising plans. In July Google announced that advertisers would be able to buy native advertising programmatically via DoubleClick Bid Manager. The DoubleClick by Google website stated at the time:

> Building your native ads in DoubleClick allows you to make your native strategy a part of your broader digital strategy, rather than having it live in a silo. You can apply DoubleClick's targeting, buying and measurement capabilities that you're accustomed to for your programmatic campaigns, to your native ads.[4]

Advertisers can now upload the 'moving parts' of a native ad – a headline, image thumbnail and description/intro text. Google then assembles these assets to the contextual look and feel of the website or app where the advertising is going to appear. It very much falls into the in-feed native distribution form of native advertising (see Chapter 6) that is the main programmatic vehicle of native advertising, too.

This is Google's first foray into native advertising; it almost certainly will not be its last. Google is undoubtedly testing the impact that allowing native advertising formats will bring: with a multi-billion-dollar search business to protect, any adjustments it makes to the buy-and-sell-side model need to be thoroughly tested for business impact.

But a buzzword native advertising is not. When Google turns its attention to any aspect of digital, it's time for everyone to sit up and take notice. So if an endorsement for the business opportunity around native advertising was ever needed, this is it.

10 ways programmatic native advertising will change advertising

Many marketers are often left confused by programmatic advertising, fearful of the complexity, scale and targeting at their fingertips, but there are major benefits to programmatic. Programmatic native advertising will transform the digital campaigns of the future. Here's how:

1 Native advertising will form part of an overall digital strategy

New advertising formats can and do sometimes run in isolation to overall campaigns. There are many reasons for this: test budgets sometimes operate outside of campaign objectives; advertisers don't like to rely on new formats for key strategic campaigns. Programmatic native advertising means that rolling native advertising into any and every digital campaign is easier. Native advertising no longer has to live in its own 'content' or 'native' silo. It can be incorporated into all digital plans easily.

2 Mobile programmatic native advertising

Programmatically traded native advertising will see an explosion in the number of native ad campaigns running on mobile. Native advertising is undoubtedly the ideal format for mobile. Feeds, as we've demonstrated earlier, are fast becoming the most effective way for brands to distribute content: mobile advertising is all about the feed.

3 Data will continue to grow in importance

Real-time buying and selling brings data opportunities to the fore for native advertising in an entirely new way. Programmatic advertising means that data will be standardized across formats – video, display and native – which will increasingly draw ever more favourable comparisons for native ad formats.

4 Transparency will become even more important

Programmatic trading allows innumerable economies of scale. Ads are served to audience, as well as publishers and publisher verticals – in real time. But with this scale comes the question of transparency. The market will need to enforce and ensure that brand safety concerns are met if it is going to maximize the programmatic native opportunity.

5 Viewability will become an increasing issue

Just as transparency around the publisher environment is important, so too is viewability. Was that native ad actually seen? What constitutes an engagement? These questions will become key for programmatic native advertising in order to win over its detractors and to minimize the disruption of potential ad fraud. Sophisticated measurement tools will grow in importance as they will be used to verify quality and confirm delivery of advertising.

6 The creative approval process will evolve

Content is at the core of native advertising. As publishers open up their inventory to programmatic native ads, the industry needs to develop approval processes – and in fact is already developing measures that allow for publisher approval of native ad campaigns. This will be paramount to allay publisher concerns of programmatic marketplaces and inappropriate advertising appearing on their publications.

7 Publishers will become ad tech experts

As native advertising increasingly goes programmatic, the tech expertise of publishers will grow. More and more publishers will need to invest in expertise – and work with bespoke native ad platforms – in order to unbox the opportunities for increased ad revenue. This will require more and more expertise sitting 'in-house' at publishers, who understand programmatic technologies such as header bidding, server-to-server, private marketplaces, programmatic guaranteed and more of what they need to do to maximize the programmatic opportunity for their inventory. There is currently a very real lack in skilled programmatic expertise across the ad industry, both on the buy and sell side. This is an area that the industry will need to address swiftly in the years ahead.

8 Timing will be everything

Programmatic native advertising opens the door to real-time bidding across an entire swathe of native ad inventory previously not accessible. Real-time bidding will mean that timing will become increasingly important for running native ad campaigns. Content, image and video optimization, performed in real time, will increasingly be responsible for meeting campaign KPIs.

9 We will have more time for creativity

As advertisers have more time to think about strategy and overall campaign objectives, creativity will naturally increase. Native advertising is arguably the most creative digital ad format that's been developed. The content opportunities are endless, but the scalable technology and real-time bidding of programmatic ensure that there will be few technological or audience limitations to those creative ideas. We have only just scratched the surface.

10 *We will have more time to focus on the big picture*

Programmatic native advertising promises to do much of the 'heavy lifting' of running a native ad campaign. Currently, most advertisers juggle numerous publishers, platforms and creative assets when running native campaigns. This programmatic approach should make much of these commercial and campaign processes uniform, ideally leaving marketers with more time to think strategically and objectively.

Summary

Programmatic native advertising is still very much in its infancy. But much of the technological 'plumbing' required to make native advertising work programmatically is now complete. This opens the door for more and more display money – which is primarily bought and sold programmatically nowadays – to move directly into native advertising formats. Programmatic is unifying the way digital advertising is bought and sold and is without a doubt the future of trading in all advertising. Technology and formats will continue to evolve, allowing ever more campaign optimization and targeting to take place alongside maximizing scale. Yes, programmatic has its challenges, many of which we have discussed in earlier chapters, but at its heart it is just a tool – albeit an extremely powerful, profitable one – which, once advertisers and publishers understand how to use more effectively, will be embraced fully by all marketers.

Endnotes

1 Marshall, J (20 February 2014) Digiday. WTF is programmatic advertising? [online] http://digiday.com/media/what-is-programmatic-advertising [accessed 25 May 2017]

2 Brierley, K (22 February 2017) Business.com. Programmatic What? A Comparison of Programmatic Buying and the Stock Market [online] www.business.com/articles/programmatic-buying-and-the-stock-market/ [accessed 25 May 2017]

3 Low, KW (20 March 2017) Nativo partners with The Trade Desk to offer native ads programmatically [online] http://laadtech.com/?p=370 [accessed 25 May 2017]

4 DoubleClick by Google (July 2016) Build beautiful ads at scale: Programmatic native in DoubleClick bid manager [online] www.doubleclickbygoogle.com/articles/programmatic-native-ads-beautiful-creative-doubleclick-bid-manager/ [accessed 25 May 2017]

The next generation of native advertising

16

We have covered in earlier sections of this book how the native advertising market is going to grow over the next few years. In Chapter 5 we looked at how the global native ad market will be worth more than $85 billion by 2020. We've looked at how the growth in mobile browsing, branded content and the ubiquity of video advertising, as well as the leap to programmatic buying models and changing consumer attitudes to advertising, will all play their part in this phenomenal growth. I'm confident that this is going to happen. The path for native advertising growth is set – and the market, by and large, is following it.

In this chapter we'll touch upon some of the changes we can expect to see over the next few years. This chapter will focus more on what native advertising could become in the longer term: what will native advertising look like in 10 years' time, for example, or even in 15–20 years' time? It's a challenge to predict. But it is an important exercise to carry out. Why? Because I think only by looking at the past, present and, indeed, what the future could be, is it possible to fully understand native advertising as a whole.

Only by looking forward can we reinforce what is a known truth in the digital world: nothing stays the same; everything changes. What is now, will tomorrow be in the past. The ideas and tips I've shared with you in this book will almost certainly be rendered obsolete in the years ahead by new ways of thinking, new products and, as British Prime Minister Harold MacMillan famously said, 'events, dear boy, events'.[1] But I don't mean to say this to deter you. I want to highlight that native advertising will continually progress.

It will continue to evolve, and splinter into ever more categories and sub-categories for as long as there is digital advertising. But if you can see how this evolution has happened – and understand from the past where the change in the future may come – you will be well equipped to benefit from it. You may even be in a great position to create the next evolution of native advertising yourself. You may recognize a new category, a new business angle that uses technology to offer something new and creative to an advertising market that is always looking for innovation and product differentiation.

So here's a brief summary of what the future of native advertising may look like.

Enter the gold rush: native advertising booms

Native advertising has completed its 'proof of concept' phase. Marketers increasingly get it – and are responding by increasing budgets. Advances in the buying and selling process, championed by programmatic native advertising, will make it easier for brand budgets to find their ways into native advertising formats. Scale will grow as display advertising units diminish, and mobile native advertising will become the largest digital ad format in existence. Likewise, publishers' own brand content solutions and publisher partnership offerings will become ever more popular as advertisers become more familiar with the offering and the benefits. Globally, the market will grow everywhere, and by the end of the five-year period will come to dominate digital marketing spend.

Brand differentiators and subtle tech innovation to platform and product will be everywhere, but a key trend in native advertising in the immediate future will be the adoption of artificial intelligence (AI).

Money enters the market

As more money flows into the market, more and more players will enter the field. This will leave some customers confused. This will fuel a growing need for clearer recognition of the different native product categories in existence. More and more often the market will need to reference and fall back on these definitions and categories of native advertising in order to feel comfortable with the product. Luckily, we've simplified these categories of native advertising in earlier chapters.

There will be a glut of new native advertising businesses entering the field. Most will be ex-display ad networks rebranding as native advertising businesses – chasing the market for success (this is already happening, but it will increase). There's a danger that these ex-display networks could damage the native market if they enter it incorrectly, leaving both advertisers and media owners jaded.

The display networks that make the transition successfully to native advertising will have to buy or merge with established native advertising businesses in order to gain market share, experience, respectability and to harness their unique market expertise. It will be the responsibility of existing native advertising businesses, which helped pioneer the format and market, to help reinforce acceptable standards, ways of working and drive innovation:

- The large digital players, notably Google and Facebook, will continue to advance their own versions of native advertising.
- Hybrid business models, where agencies and publishers increasingly invest in native ad tech, distribution and native content businesses, will increase. These businesses will try to figure out ways to minimize risks to their existing business models, and/or maximize from content marketing growth and the burgeoning native advertising market.

The market will be ripe for consolidation

Well-backed businesses will emerge to challenge and 'own' specific categories and sub-categories of native advertising. Some of these businesses are already in existence today, of course – a source of untapped native advertising potential for investors – but there are also any number of new, as yet unlaunched native businesses waiting in the wings.

What will the market look like?

What the native advertising landscape will look like afterwards is not clear. Will there be one large digital advertising behemoth that 'owns' a particular facet of native advertising by 2022? Will it be in a position to challenge the duopoly of Google and Facebook? Or will native advertising simply be sequestered by the existing dominant businesses in digital? Or will publishers fiercely withstand any attempts to commoditize their unique native advertising offerings and be able to fight a rear-guard action – possibly using some as yet undefined technology, business model or product – in order to flourish? Could the 'flight to quality' signal a renaissance in publishing for successful heritage brands with native advertising at its heart?

Time will tell. But over the intervening years we can expect the market to change, challenger brands to appear and consolidation to take place.

The growth in artificial intelligence

Artificial intelligence (AI) is already big news in digital marketing. While many of the mainstream media stories you see about AI tend to focus on the negatives – job losses, poor customer experience, programming mistakes – the media and marketing industries are typically more upbeat about AI – especially digital marketers. For an industry that is built on technology and the possibility of scale, the benefits of AI are somewhat obvious. The automation of any process via machine learning – effectively so that a specific task is completed more efficiently in terms of time, and more accurately, than a human could do it – is exciting. There are many examples in digital of how AI is slowly being used. In e-commerce, numerous businesses have developed chatbots to assist in customer service operations and product recommendation. The products are continually tested, improved upon and re-launched to specification. Few people in marketing doubt that they will not get better over time.

Chatbots, AI and content recommendation

Chatbots are increasingly being used by publishers to share and promote content. In March 2016, Outbrain launched 'Outbrain for Chat',[2] a service that is intended to allow any of its publishers to launch 'content bots' across leading messaging platforms such as Facebook chat in minutes. It's what Outbrain have dubbed 'conversational content', which combines personalized recommendations and editorial controls within chat applications. The technology in use has AI included and is dynamic, so it learns over time what content users like, promising to present users with the latest news and most interesting stories. Users can view, save for later or read the articles within the messaging app, plus much more.

In November 2016, Outbrain announced it would launch personalized, private messagechat bots via Outbrain for Chat on messaging apps such as Facebook Messenger in partnership with Time Inc. The plans announced that it would launch news, information and lifestyle content to readers of People, Variety, NME, Sky News and the Nikkei Asian Review in the US, UK and Japan respectively.[3]

Outbrain believes that messaging is a key future platform, where audiences will spend more and more of their digital lives. Messaging apps will increasingly become new browsers and chatbots will replace existing websites and many apps. Outbrain for Chat is the company's attempt to innovate the delivery of native content within what it describes as a 'new medium'.

Native advertising targeting and AI

While companies such as Outbrain are creating new AI learning tools to target emerging new mediums such as messaging, more and more businesses are looking to improve the delivery of advertising messages on existing platforms, too. The opportunity afforded by AI in native advertising delivery is significant. By introducing machine learning and deep scanning of pages, the level of targeting available to advertisers for particular campaigns can be ever more granular.

In an ad medium where context is everything, the more data – and learnings from that data – you can garner in real time, autonomously, the greater the likely performance. Native advertising is all about being in the middle of a content feed and highly visible. The power comes from the editorial content and the native ad endorsing each other. In other types of digital ads, such as banners, the ad placement is next to the editorial content and not inside. Content and ads stand at a defined place and don't endorse each other, which makes contextualization less critical. In classic display advertising, such as banners, contextualization is a nice-to-have. For native ads it's a must-have, and advertisers have been asking for that for a long time. It's a potential game-changer for native advertising that is run programmatically.

IBM Watson and AI

No mention of AI is complete without mention of IBM Watson. Named after IBM's first CEO Thomas J. Watson, who turned the company into the global business empire we know today, Watson is a cognitive technology that can think like a human. In more tech-speak, it is question answering (QA) technology that deeply analyses the content of natural language questions to answer those questions with precision. In order to do this Watson has roughly 200 million pages of natural language content that it can call upon – equivalent to reading 1 million books.

It is part of a longstanding tradition at IBM in terms of developing unique computer science tools. In 1997 the company's Deep Blue chess-playing system successfully beat world chess champion Gary Kasparov. Watson is a result of IBM's attempt to compete and beat the human champions of US TV quiz show *Jeopardy!* In February 2011, Watson competed in and won the $1 million prize money on the show.

IBM has made Watson technology available for any number of different business uses via a series of APIs (application programming interface). Many AI initiatives in the world of health, science, engineering and entertainment are powered by IBM Watson.

In advertising terms, in July 2016 IBM announced that it was going to use Watson for all of its future programmatic native advertising buying by the end of the year – a marketing spend of potentially more than $50 million a year. In January 2017, IBM announced that it is also rolling out the technology to media buying in the UK.

IBM Watson and native advertising

In October 2016, I was privileged enough to be part of the business that brought the first AI semantic targeting capability to native advertising, when ADYOULIKE integrated Watson into its native advertising platform. My role was limited, I have to admit; much of that credit should go to Julien Verdier, CEO, ADYOULIKE, and our formidable tech team. But it was very exciting to be a part of it.

As part of the integration, Watson scans all of the publisher pages across the ADYOULIKE global network of premium publishers and analyses them in the same way a human mind would: looking contextually for topics, sentiment and semantics rather than just scanning for simple keywords.

This allows advertisers to deliver native content in-feed in the most relevant and targeted way possible. Watson looks at where, why and how the existing editorial content on each site is 'talking about' subjects and ensures advertisers are dynamically delivering the best native content to fit.

The Watson AI can look at existing content in a way that was previously impossible, providing a wealth of contextual data that examines not just what a publisher is writing about, but why. We are now able, in real time, to associate any kind of advertising content to the best matching editorial context, whatever the level of semantic targeting expected by advertisers and publishers. That makes it an invaluable tool for native advertising.

It is unlikely ADYOULIKE will be the only business doing this soon. But it's nice to be first.

As marketers, we now have so much access to data that how we decide to use and analyse that data most effectively and craft compelling content that plays to those insights, in real-time scenarios, can only really be done at scale by some form of AI. On this reasoning, AI will become an increasingly common part of the native advertising landscape of the future, as it combines with AI advances in the programmatic buying space to improve relevance, targeting and performance for advertisers.

2030: a glimpse of native advertising in the future

While the next decade or so of native advertising may well be characterized by much of the above, as we near the end of this book, I want to offer a glimpse of the direction in which native advertising – in fact digital advertising as a whole – may be heading.

There are a few key trends of note that continue to get tech evangelists excited; and wherever new technology appears and consumers run to embrace it, you can guarantee that ad-led business models will follow. Increasingly these ad models will be evolved native advertising formats.

Riding the crest of the third wave

Key factors that will impact our lives over the next decades include: automation, artificial intelligence, virtual reality, augmented reality and the Internet of Things. These are huge topics worthy of their own books, so I will not go into exacting detail here about each and every one of them. But their impact will increasingly be felt as we go about our daily lives. They will bring about fundamental changes in consumer behaviour and expectation.

The digital domain that we, as marketers, operate in will face continued and rapid change as we adjust to the awesome power of these new technologies. Consumer habits will change rapidly, placing ever more opportunity – and challenges – for marketers to embrace. These technologies will certainly be used by enterprising marketers to continue their quest for deeper relationships with their intended audiences.

Many of these technologies are already here, of course. But in a decade or so they'll be ubiquitous.

Virtual reality and augmented reality become reality

Virtual reality is growing in popularity. By the end of 2016, there were estimated to be more than 6 million virtual reality (VR) users worldwide, according to data from Deutsche Bank;[4] 50 million people had downloaded the Google Cardboard App by May 2016, 25 million of them since January 2016.[5] Pokemon Go, the highly addictive game that enthralled the world in the summer of 2016, was, for millions, their first foray into the world of augmented reality (AR). It will not be their last. Momentum is growing around these technologies – and entrepreneurial businesses are poised to push this tech from 'early adopter' products to mass market in the coming years. It is going to happen.

VR and AR are areas worth mentioning in relation to native advertising adoption in particular. Why? Because when you hear Mark Zuckerberg say things like, 'VR is going to be the most social platform',[6] and when Facebook unveils its 10-year roadmap with entire sections dedicated to AI and VR/AR,[7] you simply have to sit up and take notice as a digital marketer. It's significant.

Think a little bit about what Facebook and Mark Zuckerberg are saying here: VR is the next big thing. OK. VR could overtake the existing social media model. That's big news, isn't it? Now think about it from another angle. Facebook currently makes billions and billions of ad dollars from the existing social media model. If they are going to champion the emergence of a new 'form of media' as Dillon Seo, CEO of VoleR Creative and Co-Founder of Oculus describes VR, you can be pretty sure that they are also going to champion and promote a form of advertising on that media that makes it easy for their existing customer base to easily buy into and promote their products on there too. That's simple business acumen. What form will advertising on VR platforms take? An incarnation of native advertising.

The rise of immersive media experiences

We live increasingly in an immersive, media-driven world. 360 videos, photos and computer games, as well as VR and AR, mean that more and more often as consumers we expect an immersive media experience. Immersive media is defined as digital technology, content or images that deeply involve one's senses and may create an altered mental state.

Engagement is used a lot in modern marketing. We are always looking to engage our customer's time, engage them with exciting content. Engagement is great, but immersion is what everyone will aim for in the future. The former takes place when a marketing message provokes some sort of action among an audience – a share, a tweet or an endorsement to a friend. Immersion is when you forget the message entirely, forget you are the audience even, and instead fall into a newly manufactured reality.

Immersion really does blur the lines between story and marketing, storyteller and audience, illusion and reality. A Mindshare Trends report from 2015 found that, as consumers, we increasingly 'crave immersive and sensory experiences that completely absorb our attention and help us feel real again'.[8] Why? I'm not so sure, but in an age where we are bombarded with messages, notifications and updates 24/7, perhaps it's a craving we have to be so overwhelmed by an experience, that we actually switch off and live in the moment for a time? Absorbed in the story we are being told.

By breaking the 'fourth wall' and commanding our attention fully – 100 per cent of the time, where second screening is an impossibility – the ability to create and tell truly immersive stories can be extremely powerful. From a brand point of view, these immersive experiences can help build a shortcut to empathy, cultivate deep emotions of affection and foster high levels of brand recall. The opportunities are endless.

It is this quest for immersion that will become the dominant fixation of marketers in the future. Data and creativity will combine ever more. The tools to build these immersive realities will be available to them.

Down the rabbit hole into a brave new world of immersion

Imagine if you had told a marketer back in 1984 that in the future they'd be able to write an advertising message, or piece of content, and share it – at the click of just a few buttons – with an audience of potentially millions, who could read, share, visit and buy your products from a handheld phone. And in order to do this you would not have to leave your desk, or even speak to anyone else. You could do it all from your computer. Instantly. You'd be naturally greeted with disbelief. Fast-forward a couple of decades or so from now and think the inconceivable.

By 2030 – or even sooner – marketers will have immersive generating tools at their fingertips that we can only dream of today. Social networks – and the feed as a whole – will become gateways to immersive new worlds that we'll continually dip in and out of. A lot of these tools will likely sit within social network 'walled gardens'; but there will undoubtedly be independent tools, too. Marketing strategies will focus on how to 'invite' audiences into these worlds via the feed. Immersion and brand messaging will increasingly take place inside these brand-created, or brand-hosted, worlds.

In the future, VR will enable even more types of connection — like the ability for friends who live in different parts of the world to spend time together and feel like they're really there with each other.

The VR brand environment of the future

Imagine these connections with friends and family happening in an environment that was created by a brand. Friends living in far-flung countries meeting up in a virtual 'bar room', 'hosted' by Heineken or Budweiser, for example, to watch the latest football match; a family reunion in a cosy living room created by Nestle, Unilever or Procter & Gamble; or a group of friends partying to the latest Rihanna concert within a Sony, Nike or Red Bull themed environment. It would all feel very real. The emotion, the connection, the memories will be real – the immersive interaction with a brand full on. Within these VR rooms, AI would be used to crunch the data that these virtual world conversations and interactions create in real time, giving brands invaluable data points that they can use to add to the conversation – subtly, and in ways we can only just imagine. It wouldn't be the hard sell, more like a friend recommending something to you as it comes up in conversation.

Let's take the football example and run with it. We have a group of old school friends from London, now flung across the world living in Singapore, Japan, India, Australia and the US. They are big football fans and they decide to come together and meet up for the latest Arsenal v Chelsea football match. The game starts, conversation flows. It becomes quickly obvious to anyone involved – including the AI monitoring the chat – that the group are all Arsenal fans. A simple tactic at half-time, then, would mean that instead of showing generic ads on the screen, the ads would be far more targeted towards the audience – not just towards Arsenal fans, but Arsenal fans who live in Singapore, Japan, India, Australia and the US, as well as hundreds of other data points accessible to the platform in order to identify the likes, dislikes, needs and desires of each person. Each of them will see a different set of ads, depending on their own data.

So far, so similar to modern targeting in digital. But in an immersive brand world you can do much, much more. What if, as part of the immersive room the beer brand have created, they had an entire 'back catalogue' of ex-Arsenal players – every squad member still alive since 1990, for example, watching the game, too. The role of these ex-players is to 'float' around the numerous immersive rooms, popping in to watch some of the game alongside this group of mates. So when the second half kicks off Ian Wright, Thierry Henry or Dennis Bergkamp are there too, just popping into the 'bar room' to say hello and 'shake hands' with everyone. The group are completely immersed: they've all just met one of their heroes. It's a great story they are going to share with their mates again and again. You know where they are going to watch the next game, too, don't you?

Who made that possible for them? The brand of course. Now that's immersion. That's building a brand narrative in a unique and extraordinary way. That's the fusion of creativity, technology, data and ideas to tell a story – not a spoon-fed story created by the brand for consumers to passively consume, but rather creating an environment and opportunity for your target audience to create their own positive stories in a brand environment.

This is just one kind of example of the future of digital advertising experience we are likely to see as AI, VR and AR develop and become permanent fixtures in our daily lives and the toolkits of marketers the world over. It will be a new form of media, yes, but native advertising – in a new incarnation – will form much of the advertising model underpinning it.

Endnotes

1 Dilks, D (1993) *Office of Prime Minister in Twentieth Century Britain*, Hull University Press, Hull

2 Outbrain (24 March 2016) Outbrain unveils 'Outbrain for Chat' [online] www.outbrain.com/about/press/outbrain-for-chat [accessed 29 March 2017]

3 Doody, C (22 November 2016) Outbrain evolves Outbrain for Chat to deliver the smartest experience, a look how [online] hwww.outbrain.com/blog/outbrain-evolves-outbrain-for-chat [accessed 26 May 2017]

4 eMarketer (11 May 2016) Media companies tap virtual reality to drive immersive experiences [online] www.emarketer.com/Article/Media-Companies-Tap-Virtual-Reality-Drive-Immersive-Experiences/1013942 [accessed 29 March 2017]

5 Matey, L (18 May 2017) Google Cardboard platform picks up steam with 50M app downloads to date [online] https://techcrunch.com/2016/05/18/google-cardboard-platform-picks-up-steam-with-50m-app-downloads-to-date/ [accessed 29 March 2017]

6 Chaykowski, K (24 February 2016) Mark Zuckerberg has a plan to bring Facebook users into virtual reality [online] www.forbes.com/sites/kathleenchaykowski/2016/02/24/mark-zuckerberg-has-a-plan-to-make-virtual-reality-social/#24702d7331f1 [accessed 29 March 2017]

7 D'Onfro, J (12 April 2016) Facebook just showed us its 10-year road map in one graphic [online] http://uk.businessinsider.com/facebook-f8-ten-year-roadmap-2016-4 [accessed 29 March 2017]

8 Mindshare (2015) Mindshare Trends 2015 [online] www.mindshareworld.com/sites/default/files/Mindshare%20Trends%202015_1.pdf [accessed 29 March 2017]

Conclusion: a call to arms 17

As I set out in the introduction to this book, I am of the opinion that native advertising is more than just a new, convenient advertising format. I believe that what we are seeing is the evolution of online advertising – how it is created and consumed – and that native advertising is the first truly native-to-digital ad format in existence.

Native advertising has risen out of the primordial swamp of competing online advertising formats that characterized the first 20 years or so of the internet and is evolving – thanks to its fluidity, accessibility and innovation – to become the dominant form of digital advertising in existence.

It's malleable and difficult to define, yes, but this is what makes it so exciting. It can take on many guises and it happily steals and borrows from other ad formats, other online mediums – editorial, video, music, design, technology and more – to fuse itself into ever more forms. It's a chameleon and a cuckoo combined. It'll eat your lunch, but cook you dinner. Sometimes you'll love it, other times you'll dislike it. Just like the internet itself.

The people practising native advertising today are at the cutting edge of digital advertising creativity – not just in the traditional 'creative' big idea-led approach to advertising, but in the use of technology and data, too. Planner buyers, ad ops teams and programmatic executives are part of this native advertising creativity as much as copywriters, commercial editors and designers. As I explained in Chapter 10 (Building a team for native advertising success), it's about left- and right-brain thinking – but it's even more about teamwork.

Native advertising sits in the cross-hairs of art and science, creativity and data. It's a tool, a canvas and an opportunity for all to flex their imaginations within clear commercial objectives. Native advertising is the format of choice for experimentation in digital advertising today. There's no excuse for poor ideas in digital any longer. From idea to execution, analysis to results, it's far far easier than it's ever been to be creative at scale – and achieve commercial objectives.

This is my call to arms to everyone in digital advertising today: use this tool, nurture it, experiment with it, and bend it to your requirements. Think big, or think small, but don't be boring. Test, test and test some more – the rewards are enormous, the opportunity waiting.

To me the rise of native advertising is inevitable. I could be biased, of course. You've read this far. What do you think?

Feel free to continue the conversation with me at:

Twitter @DaleL_NativeAds

LinkedIn www.linkedin.com/in/dalelovell

INDEX

Italics indicate a figure or table in the text.